Open My Eyes
LORD

Open My Eyes
LORD

Erica Kim

DPI
DISCIPLESHIP
PUBLICATIONS
INTERNATIONAL

www.dpibooks.org

Open My Eyes, Lord
©2009 by DPI Books
5016 Spedale Court #331
Spring Hill, TN 37174

All Scripture quotations, unless indicated, are taken from
the NEW INTERNATIONAL VERSION.
Copyright ©1973, 1978, 1984 by the International Bible Society.
Used by permission of Zondervan Publishing House.
All rights reserved.

The "NIV" and "New International Version" trademarks
are registered in the United States Patent Trademark Office
by the International Bible Society.
Use of either trademarks requires the permission of
the International Bible Society.

Printed in the United States of America

Cover Design: Brian Branch
Cover Photo: ©istockphoto.com/zoomstudio
Interior Design: Thais Gloor

ISBN: 978-1-57782-239-4

To my two spiritual heroes,
George and Irene Gurganus.
They have fought the good fight
and see clearly what I long to see.

CONTENTS

Foreword 9

Introduction: What Is Reality? 13

Chapter 1—Spiritual Light: How Can I See When It's So Dark? 19

1. Jesus Is the Light 22
2. Trusting in Jesus Through Difficulties 26
3. Learning from Jacob 29
4. God's Purposes in His Guidance 32
5. Opportunities Through Challenges 34
6. Remembering the Cross of Christ 35

Chapter 2—Satan: Does He Have Power Over Me? 41

1. Who Has the Power in This World? 41
2. How Did Satan Come About? 45
3. Satan's Weapons for Mass Destruction 47
4. Recognizing Satan's Lies....................................53
5. Preventing Ourselves from Being Deceived 55
6. Pay the Price for Truth.......................................58
7. Satan Attacks Spiritual People 63

Chapter 3—The Holy Spirit: How Does He Lead Me? 68

1. The Workings of the Spirit 68
2. Living to Please the Spirit 73
3. Learning to Be Led by the Spirit 79
4. What Happens If I Don't Follow the Spirit?......83
5. The Gifts of the Spirit 89

Chapter 4—Demons: Are These Evil Spirits Still Active Today? 95

1. Are Demons Real? 96
2. What Do They Do? 97
3. Demonic Activity...98
4. Don't Be Led Astray 102
5. Resist and Pray 106
6. Idolatry and Demons..109

Chapter 5—Angels: Are They Truly Around Me?............117

1. Angels, Cherubim, Seraphs and Archangels.....................117
2. Angels Exist Today 120
3. Angels As Our Guardians 124
4. Angels As Messengers 127
5. Angelic Intervention 134

Chapter 6—Prayer: Why Do It When God Already Knows? 143

1. Why We Need to Pray...143
2. Desperate Times Call for Desperate Measures 151
3. Don't Give Up Praying..157

Chapter 7—God's Church: Why Do I Need Family? 163

1. God Is All About Community 163
2. The Church Is a Spiritual Kingdom.................................167
3. Jesus' Sacrifice for the Church 171
4. Actively Serving in God's Community 175
5. Allowing Friendships to Keep You Faithful 179

Chapter 8—Hell: Is There Really a Place of Condemnation?..........185

1. What Is Hell?...189
2. The Two Prevalent Views of Hell 191
3. Why Would a Loving God Create Hell?............................196
4. So What If There Is a Hell? 199

Chapter 9—Heaven: Is It All That It's Built Up to Be?.....................204

1. Putting Our Hope in Heaven..204
2. Heaven Is a Real Place 210
3. Understanding the Concept of Eternity 214
4. Wait for God's Promises..220

FOREWORD

Have you ever looked for something, yet failed to see it even though it was right in front of your eyes? I have had that experience more than once when trying to find the car keys in my purse! My Texas family had an expression to fit that situation. They would say, "If it had been a snake, it would have bit you!"

In the spiritual world there are many things we do not "see," and in a manner of speaking, some of those things could bite us! In the Old Testament a prophet was also called a seer—he could see things in a spiritual way that others could not. Today we need to open our eyes to the spiritual reality around us. We cannot do that without the help of God and his word. In the sense of enlightening us and urging us to "see spiritually," Erica Kim, though not prophetically inspired, could be called a modern-day seer.

At a time when movies such as *Angels and Demons* and *Twilight* are drawing huge crowds, interest in the spiritual realm and other-worldly creatures is obvious. If there was ever a time that true biblical principles about God's spiritual world need to be presented, that time is now! Erica has taken up the challenge of addressing such controversial subjects as the role of Satan and his demons, hell and heaven, the existence of angels, and the work of the Holy Spirit. I am thankful that Erica has had the conviction and courage to delve into these deep topics to enlighten us as women in today's world.

What a joy it has been to see Erica develop from her early years as a campus student in Boston to the mature Christian woman, wife, mother and writer that she is today. God has certainly shaped her with a wide range of experiences.

With her Japanese heritage being basically nonreligious, then coming to a deep faith in Jesus and his word, she has a keen perspective of the spiritual realm. Even as a young woman Erica was seen as deeply spiritual and very aware of the spiritual influences in her life.

In her college years, Erica had a profound impact on many young women, including our three daughters. She was a friend and mentor in their lives and became like a fourth daughter to Al and me. One of the things I admire most about Erica is her diligent study of God's word and her desire for it to be the foundation of her spiritual life. And now, combining that strength with her writing talent, she will influence countless other women. This book is the compilation of many of her experiences and the application of spiritual truths she has found in the Bible.

I love the way Erica begins this book and the way she ends it. At the very beginning, she focuses us on the true Light, Jesus, to help us see even in the midst of darkness. Then she finishes the book calling us to see the reality of heaven—our eternal home as Christians.

When it comes to the spiritual world, we all have questions, many that are not easily answered. Erica does an excellent job of "book-ending" some of the more difficult spiritual subjects with the certain truths of Jesus and heaven! In between she takes us on a journey to see the spiritual world more clearly.

As we journey through the book with Erica, she doesn't leave us in the clutches of Satan, but quickly shows us through God's word how to have a close friendship with the very Spirit of God. My own awareness of God's Spirit was deepened as she reminded me that he knows us fully, accepts us, really understands us, and surrounds us with his unconditional love. The Holy Spirit is the close companion we all long for and need.

Then after looking at the darkness of demons, Erica highlights the presence and power of God's angels, strengthening our faith to see that we are not alone in this spiritual battle.

In the apostle Paul's instruction in Ephesians 6 about fighting the spiritual battle, he stated and restated the necessity of prayer. While addressing some of our common questions about prayer, Erica vulnerably shares some of the desperate times in her life and the essential part prayer played in the development of her faith.

The chapter on God's spiritual family, the church, is a vital part of seeing the true spiritual world. You may have heard a story about a little boy who was frightened by a loud thunderstorm one night. He quickly ran to get in bed with his parents, but his dad told him to go back to bed...that God would be with him.

The little boy responded, "Daddy, you go sleep with God, and I'll sleep here with Mommy—I need someone with skin on!"

All of us do need "someone with skin on"—we need each other in this spiritual battle. Erica shares a gripping story of one woman's physical life being saved through the relationships in God's family. She shows us how God continues to extend his love and protection in concrete ways through the church and through his power in the spiritual realms.

Our reality is often defined by what we see, hear and experience at any given moment. If we have difficulty seeing past our immediate situation, how much more challenging is it for us to keep a spiritual perspective. *Open My Eyes, Lord* is a great title for this book, but even more it is a needed prayer for us to pray.

Erica has masterfully interwoven her own and others' life experiences with examples from God's men like Jacob and Elisha to help us practically see the spiritual world around us.

This book will help us to be more alert to and better prepared for the battle that rages around us—the battle that ends in ultimate victory with God!

To him who is able to keep you from falling and to present you before his glorious presence without fault and with great joy—to the only God our Savior be glory, majesty, power and authority, through Jesus Christ our Lord, before all ages, now and forevermore! Amen.

Jude 24-25

Gloria Baird
June 2009

Introduction

WHAT IS REALITY?

On February 5, 1996, Mapquest.com was created as an online Internet site, providing interactive mapping services. People all over the United States and, now, around the world have benefited from the billions of maps available through this Web site—an innovative system for those who need to find directions quickly to different states and cities across their countries. As travelers, whether to near-by cities or faraway countries, we have a consistent need to identify the best route to our destinations. No wonder this company is one of the transformational stories of this generation.

In the same way, God has provided a map for every Christian. His word shows us the best path to great relationships, lasting marriages and faithful living until our final destination: heaven. It reveals truths that are crucial for Christians today and in the future.

A Christian is a traveler—a pilgrim in this world on a passage of faith. As travelers, we, too, need a map to lead us in our faith. While on this spiritual peregrination, we will experience moments of joy, pain, euphoria and despair. It is an adventure not unlike exploring the jungles of the Amazon or visiting the mysterious pyramids of Egypt, and one that will demand perseverance and trust in God.

The Bible opens up an odyssey of the unseen and intangible— for those who dare to look into its sometimes mysterious truths, it reveals answers, hope and grace. Inside its pages exists a reality that lives and breathes in a realm apart from and yet enveloping every mortal being. It is only through the eyes of faith that the clouds of obscurity can be cleared to reveal a reality that cannot be ignored.

From every passage of Scripture, God and his existence are

paired with miracles, signs and wonders. Those markers give us gauges and even warnings to carry the Christian voyager to righteous and virtuous paths. Sadly, we live in a world that leads us to believe otherwise. It is difficult for us to live against the tide. It takes great courage to live, not as the world lives, but as our Lord did. The world takes pleasure in the "here and now" while the true disciple has his hope set on eternity. God shows us his infinite wisdom in the Scriptures. His realm possesses the true paradise. None will find this hope in temporal gratifications.

> So we fix our eyes not on what is seen, but on what is unseen. For what is seen is temporary, but what *is unseen is eternal.* (2 Corinthians 4:18, emphasis added)

True faith in Jesus leads to life—eternal, breathtaking and boundless. While a simple knowledge of the Bible can help us in our infancy as disciples, it is not sufficient for a soul who seeks to know the deeper truths. In our walk with the Lord, we are given the choice of exploring and pursuing a deeper understanding of God. As we hunt for genuine treasures in God's heavenly world, we can grow in our convictions and the certainty of a reality that has always existed around us. We will no longer be controlled by the forces of evil, making us puppets on strings—influenced and directed by worldly opinions. Lyndon Johnson described puppets in the following way: "*Puppets. They simply respond to the pull of the most powerful strings.*"

Instead, as women of God, we will be able to sever the most influential strings and live solely by his everlasting word—not pulled emotionally, physically or circumstantially. Great men and women of faith such as the prophet Elisha lived against the tides of the world. While his contemporaries were blown to and fro by the ebb and flow of idolatry, Elisha stood firm on his hope and confidence in the eternal God. He was, in fact, a bridge between life and death; a light illuminating truth from lies; a source of wisdom apart from the foolishness of his era. No army, no commander and no government could prevail against the God of Elisha. His faith overcame despite the times. And we can too. Consider the following passage:

> Now the king of Aram was at war with Israel. After conferring with his officers, he said, "I will set up my camp in such and such a place."
>
> The man of God sent word to the king of Israel: "Beware of passing that place, because the Arameans are going down there." So the king of Israel checked on the place indicated by the man of God. Time and again Elisha warned the king, so that he was on his guard in such places.
>
> This enraged the king of Aram. He summoned his officers and demanded of them, "Will you not tell me which of us is on the side of the king of Israel?"
>
> "None of us, my lord the king" said one of the officers, "but Elisha, the prophet who is in Israel, tells the king of Israel the very words you speak in your bedroom."
>
> "Go, find out where he is," the king ordered, "so I can send men and capture him." The report came back: "He is in Dothan." Then he sent horses and chariots and a strong force there. They went by night and surrounded the city.
> (2 Kings 6:8-14)

The king of Aram is at war with Israel. To him this war is a physical battle, fought by means of strategy, scheme and design. On the other hand, to Elisha, a man of God, this war is on a spiritual platform where God is the ultimate authority and commander.

The king of Aram is frustrated by the fact that someone is telling his plans to the king of Israel. He believes that it is one of the commanders working under him who is revealing his plans and tactics to the enemy. One of the officers speaks up and says that it is Elisha the prophet. He suggests that Elisha knows what the king whispers in his very bedroom, a room only accessible to the king, his wives and his chosen servants. The king then sends horses, chariots and a strong force to capture this one man!

Isn't this the way we are many times? We see difficulties or obstacles and decide that we need to use more "force" or take more "control." Whether we thrust ourselves into having a busier schedule, muscle our way into getting that promotion or manipulate our spouses to get our way, we unknowingly miss the spiritual aspects of the situation. Our eyes can focus solely on the problem at hand and not on God's hand which has been working all along. Even Elisha's servant did not see the true reality of the battle that was being fought.

> When the servant of the man of God got up and went out early the next morning, an army with horses and chariots had surrounded the city. "Oh, my lord, what shall we do?" the servant asked.
>
> "Don't be afraid," the prophet answered, "Those who are with us are more than those who are with them."
>
> And Elisha prayed, "O LORD, open his eyes so he may see." Then the LORD opened the servant's eyes, and he looked and saw the hills full of horses and chariots of fire all around Elisha. (2 Kings 6:15-17)

Elijah prayed for his servant so that he would see the reality around him. As wayfarers in this world, our ability to see truth will come through God's word and through prayer. There is nothing in the world more powerful than prayer to open our eyes to the reality around us. We are bombarded and, as a result, deceived by false beliefs and values. Our society hates truth but loves lies and clever ideas. It revels in our shortcomings and in our weaknesses which cause us to doubt ourselves and, thus, question our faith.

Moreover, the daily routine of life often prevents us from recognizing the spiritual world around us. We end up relying exclusively on personal experiences and observations from magazines, TV, office gossip, school rumors and other propaganda, which keep us from noticing the miracles close ,to us—our existence, our children, our friends and so many more gifts from God. Hopefully in these pages, you can experience God's true world around you—a world you might have missed in your walk with him.

I pray that this book can deepen your prayer life and help you to see God and Jesus in a different and clearer way. I am offering you through these pages, a look at a world that you may have only heard about. It is like listening to mystery stories on a radio for years, then, suddenly, someone taking you to a wide-screen color movie theatre. Wow, what a difference between the two!

As you read these pages, I ask you to pray and to have an open mind to the Scriptures. Do not skip over the ones presented, but read them thoroughly, because it will be the Scriptures that bring the truth to light. As a traveler, do not let go of the map: the *word of God.* Keep your eyes on your guide as he guides you through your prayers. At the end of this adventure, hopefully, we will all make it to our ultimate destination and experience the true everlasting reality of God. So what are we waiting for? Let us pray for God to open the eyes of our heart.

Have a great journey!

~

STUDY QUESTIONS

Introduction: What Is Reality?

1. The beginning of this chapter describes us as travelers in this world. Our map is the word of God. God will guide us through our prayers. Hopefully, our journey will take us to our ultimate

destination. Think carefully and answer from the heart as you look at the following questions.

   a. Do you really want to see the reality of God's world?

   b. Do you base your spiritual experience on what you have seen or on what you read in God's word?

   c. What spiritual truths have you recently seen in your life?

2. Elijah prayed to God to open his servant's eyes so that he could see.

   a. How often do you pray?

   b. Do you pray to grow in your ability to see God's point of view for your life?

   c. Are you praying for others so that they can see the truth in God's word?

3. Write down five ways that you want to have your eyes opened by the Scriptures as you study this book.

1

Spiritual Light

How Can I See When It's So Dark?

> The people walking in the darkness
>   have seen a great light,
> on those living in the land of the shadow of death
>   a light has dawned.
>
> Isaiah 9:2

As newlyweds, Frank and I lived in Paris, France. What a romantic place to spend the second year of your marriage! When we arrived in that wonderful city, I was twenty-two years old, learning about married life and very pregnant. We made friends with a countless number of people while we were there. Yet of all the people, the one I remember the most was a woman named Agnès. She was already in her eighties when I met her. Despite the age difference, she became one of my dearest friends.

She had lived an amazing life as a young woman, interviewing famous people in France and in the French-speaking world, while also writing for several newspapers and magazines. She lived through both World War I and II. Tragically, when she was in her thirties, she lost her two children and her husband to bacterial meningitis.

Needless to say, she had experienced a hard life but one filled with adventure, so she loved telling me stories about her life. Now that she is gone, it is a privilege to share one of her stories in my book.

Agnès and I studied the Bible together every week for almost a year. During those studies, we divulged our secret fears, our hopes and our lives. As we began studying about Jesus being the light of the world, she revealed to me her fear of the dark. Our hearts connected as we laughed about our silly fears—even the ones we still battled with. But she also told me how she had overcome many of them throughout the years.

During one of our Bible studies, she told me a story about how her father helped her conquer her fear of the dark. She had lived out in the countryside of France as a little girl, in a small home with a white fence surrounding it—the "perfect" country home, at least to her. The evenings were dark outside with no street lights in her neighborhood. The only lights in the area would emanate from oil lamps from within the house, or from the ones that her father would carry with him.

On one particular evening, her father had just finished repainting the white fence around the house. The sun had gone down, so it had become very dark. Agnès was about ten years old at the time. Her father called her and asked her to join him outside. She assumed that her father was going to show her the newly painted fence. As soon as she went into the yard, however, her father did something that frightened her. He turned off his oil lamp. There was no other light nearby, only the stars in the sky, which were not enough to make her feel secure. She immediately grabbed her father's hand.

Then Agnès asked her father, "Papa, why did you turn off the lamp? I can't see, and I'm afraid."

Her father replied, "I want to help you to overcome your fear of the dark, my little one. You don't have to be afraid of it. It is time for you to grow out of your fears. In fact, I want you to walk by yourself with your palms out in front of you, all the way to the newly painted fence, and then come back to me. I will light up my lamp as soon as you tell me that you have reached the fence."

Agnès started shaking and replied, "I don't want to walk all by myself in the dark. I'm too scared."

Her father answered, "Your papa will be waiting right here. I'll be here no matter what. As soon as you shout 'I did it,' I will light up my lamp again, and you can come running back to me."

While shaking with fear, Agnès decided to trust her father and walked into what seemed like a dark chasm as she went toward the white fence. She felt like a stiff robot with her palms straight out in front of her. Her heart beat so thunderously that she could hear the loud reverberations ringing in her ears, blocking out the sound of her footsteps in the tall grass. After a couple of minutes—the equivalent of a million years to a frightened ten-year-old girl—Agnès felt the wet paint smear against her palms. It was cold and wet, mixing with the nervous sweat from her hands.

Instantaneously, tears of joy welled up and poured out of her eyes as she shouted to her father in a loud shrill, "I did it! I did it!" Immediately, the lamp went on, and she ran back to her father to show him her white palms, wet with paint and sweat.

It seemed like a miracle as her joy erased all her fears.

Even as Agnès recounted the memory from so many years ago, she had tears in her eyes—a memory of her loving father who had long since passed away. That event had occurred well over seventy years before. Yet, she recalled the moment as if it had happened that day. Her father was a light in her life. He had been a guide to eradicating so many of her fears and taught her valuable lessons, lasting her whole lifetime.

As she finished her story, she encouraged me not to fear what I could not see. Throughout her life, she had overcome her fears by picturing her father standing behind her, waiting with his lamp ready to be lit again.

1

Jesus Is the Light

The gospel or "good news" begins with Jesus. God's story is all about Jesus. Everything in the Old Testament is a preparation for us to see the true light of Christ. Seeing the light is seeing God and our Lord Jesus Christ. He is our lamp and our guide. As our soul travels in this dark world, Jesus provides the light so we can see.

Some of us may not have been raised by supportive fathers, but our God in heaven is a father who is always there for us, helping us with our fears and showing us the way. While some of our uncertainties might last an entire lifetime, God is always there to light his lamp in order to guide us through all our troubles and phobias. He not only guides, but he shows us the approach to conquer the obstacles in our lives.

We women have many fears. Some of us are good at hiding them, while others of us wear our fears in every aspect of our lives. It might not be a fear of the dark, but a fear of the future, our children's future, financial instability, or a fear of revealing our true self to others. Our fears become more apparent when we go through hard times. Like a pot of boiling stew, all the ingredients of the mixture bubble to the top. In the same way, our anxieties and our worries surface when we go through hard times.

How do you find yourself responding in times of crisis? Do you freeze up? Do you fight back? Do you run away? Do you ignore the problems and hope that they disappear? Or do you lose all hope and give up trying? Are there friends you can run to and get help, or do you hide in a shell, hoping that no one will see your failures? What role does your faith in God play at those times? Do you turn to him, or do you allow bitterness to grow in your heart as you blame him for the difficulties in your life?

Most of us have experienced difficulties and suffering. It is a part of life. We, as Christians, have a light in our lives that helps us to see through the challenges in life. Some of those trials may be small, but others may seem almost impossible for us to overcome. Take heart, Jesus is the light of the world. Even in the darkest and most bleak moments, his light is able to shine—bright enough to bring life back into our suffering hearts. The key is seeing that light and believing that it is there behind us, beside us, above us and ahead of us. Often, during these miserable times, we lose that belief and faith and, thus, fail to see the light of the Lord.

We can have many lamps in a dark room, but if we do not turn them on, they remain useless. But when we turn on the lamps, we will be able to see. In the same way, we can be Christians groping in the darkness of our faithlessness when we stop relying on God. Every fiber in us might be crying out, telling us to depend on the Lord, but we are too afraid or doubtful to let go of our fears. As a result, instead of turning on the "light of God," we continue to search for answers in the wrong places.

Every so often, God puts us in situations where we have no choice but to rely on him. We learn what it is to surrender to God's will and become living sacrifices, holy and pleasing to God—thus able to test and approve what God's will is (Romans 12:1–2). His will is never evil—but full of goodness and purpose.

As living sacrifices, our altar of surrender may be to deny negative thinking. Such thoughts do not come from the light of Jesus but from the darkness of Satan. When negative attitudes try to control us, we must take a hold of our faith and refuse to let them have power over us. The "spiritual lamps" in our hearts are turned off when we allow pessimism, cynicism and even critical feelings to rule. When the challenges come, who are you relying on for your strength? What kind of negative thinking blinds you the most? Worry? Stress? Anger? Fear?

Jesus said, "For a brief time still, the light is among you. Walk by the light you have so darkness doesn't destroy you. If you walk in darkness, you don't know where you're going. (John 12:36, The Message)

Jesus wants us to put our trust in the light. He does not want us to stumble in the darkness. He wants us to see the light clearly and to dwell within it. His path is true and eternal. In the midst of our dark despair, we need to remember to turn to God just as the great heroes in the Bible who struggled but had victories with their faith. There are also many Christians around us who have been great examples in overcoming challenges as well.

When we suffer, it can feel like our "momentary afflictions" are endless. In fact, some of these troubles can last for months or years. Others can last a lifetime. Yet, from God's perspective, these troubles are temporary when they are measured against eternity. However long or short our troubles may last, they form an important component in our spiritual walk with God. Experiencing suffering teaches us to fight against anger, guilt and bitterness. It brings every Christian to her knees in reliance on God. Sometimes, it takes terrible or tragic events for a Christian to "wake up" and go to God. In these ways, suffering teaches us to go to the light.

Fears can clamp down like a vise grip during tough times. We think of all the terrible outcomes rather than the positive possibilities. Negative thinking seizes us and our faith goes out the door. Obscurity sets in without any vision of hope and escape. It seems as if life is normal for everyone else except for us. Questions flood our minds: "Why me?" "How can this be?" "What is God trying to show me?" "Am I being punished?" Confusion begins to overtake our hearts, and we often get paralyzed in our distress.

A close Christian friend of mine named Laura was "happily" married only to find out that her husband had given in to a life of partying and being with other women after only two years of marriage. She and her husband had both become Christians while dating, then had gotten married soon afterwards and had a son. When their little boy was two years old, Laura became aware of problems in their marriage (which actually had begun during her pregnancy).

After becoming Christians, they had overcome different obstacles in their marriage, and their lives had been transformed for the better, at first. But when Laura's husband had an affair, it was a shock to her. Sadly, he never owned up to actually having an affair and continued to go out with many women during that time. He lied to Laura off and on as to whether or not he had slept with them. Although Laura made many heroic efforts to salvage their relationship—through marriage and personal counseling—her life was turned upside-down when her husband finally decided to leave her anyway.

When Laura saw that she could do nothing more to win her husband back, she gave in and decided to divorce her husband for the sake of her son. At first, Laura's husband would not agree to the divorce, because he wanted to have his fun and keep the door open to come back. All the while, her then husband continued to live a sinful life and decided to leave God. In the end, Laura divorced him and began a new life with her son.

During this time, Laura clung to God and, instead of becoming bitter and angry, she grew stronger in her relationship with him. Laura raised her son as a single mother for almost two years before she remarried a committed Christian man who was working in the ministry. Three months after they were married, Laura joined him to work on ministry staff of their church. Thankfully, her new husband is a powerful man of God who has been faithful and devoted to Laura and her now teenage son.

Laura had times when she had to fight against fear and panic about her future, especially when she saw her life and marriage crumbling before her eyes. But she learned to let Jesus light the way in the dark times. Counseling and guiding others who go through similar challenges, she now lives a life devoted to her family and to the many people in her congregation. She has been an example to me of perseverance and trust in God. I am glad to say that she is truly happily married with three wonderful children. And she would say so too!

In any of life's turmoil, Jesus is standing with his lamp ready to light our way and to show us the path. It may not seem apparent at the time, but his lamp is bright and is able to shine through—past the uncertainty, beyond the confusion and straight to the center of all our fears. His light is not an outward change of our situation but a transformation of our hearts. It is a hope that can see through even the darkest phase of our lives.

2

Trusting in Jesus Through Difficulties

Suffering. Pain. Affliction. Distress. These are experiences that we avoid because we do not want to have to face hardships in our lives. Unfortunately, life is full of these unpleasant times. Though we do not see it clearly at the time, God has his purposes and his reasons for allowing such events. We may never really understand the nature or reason for our tough times, but we can learn many valuable lessons from them. They can be used as a tool to mature us spiritually. Experiencing such times can also enable us to sympathize and emphasize with others who are going through similar situations involving weakness and pain.

Some very good friends of ours named Chaz and Ginger had been married for ten years and had unexplained fertility problems. After several years of treatment, they were overjoyed to have a positive result. Moreover, they were excited to find out that they were going to have twins. When she was at fifteen weeks, one night at midnight, Ginger's water broke. The doctor told her to go immediately to the emergency room.

Upset and confused, Chaz and Ginger went to the hospital feeling hopeful about the outcome. But when they spoke with the doctor, they were shocked to find out that the pregnancy was over. The doctor sent her home with antibiotics and ordered bed rest for her. When they returned home, they prayed for a miracle. But two days later, Ginger's fever spiked, and she went into labor. Chaz says:

> Later that night after running blood tests and ultra-sounds, Ginger and both babies were in danger. I was faced with the hardest decision of my life, which wasn't much of a choice. Baby Alexander died, and Ginger's blood test showed she was highly infected and could be battling for her life. Baby Bodie was okay, but was fighting the same infection.
>
> I had to talk over the phone with a doctor whom I had never met prior to or since then. He spelled out what everything meant in medical terms. I was frustrated because I was not a doctor and just wanted the answer.
>
> He eventually told me the only way out was to save Ginger because in another twenty-four hours she would be fighting for her life. So at 8 AM, instead of going to work, I held my son, Bodie, who had just died. At 10 AM, Ginger was still battling for her life. It still makes me cry just thinking about it, and about her courage. She was so strong and beautiful. I'm crying again, but it's okay. I need to remember sometimes.

During the labor, Ginger almost lost her life because of excessive bleeding. There are no words or answers that can be given to anyone going through such unbearable hardship. It seems so unfair to see dear friends endure such heartbreaking experiences. They prayed daily to overcome, and God was faithful to them. They were strengthened through their love for God and through the help of friends in their church. They demonstrated incredible faith as their hopes are not found in this world, but in heaven, where they will see their little boys someday, running to welcome them into God's heavenly kingdom. With that hope in their hearts, they continued to persevere in their faith.

God was faithful to their incessant prayers. Although many people do not experience happy endings after tragedies, God healed Chaz and Ginger's heart through a victory of hope and faith. Almost two years after losing their twins, Ginger was given a special gift—a surprise pregnancy! On the day of her fifteenth spiritual birthday, she gave birth to a healthy baby boy. He was born just a couple of months before this book went to the publisher.

Though Chaz and Ginger were fortunate enough to have been given a new baby, the mourning and deep pain they underwent through a miscarriage and the loss of their twins was agonizing for them. No child can replace one that has been lost.

As challenging as it may seem, God calls us to a higher plane of faith through our times of suffering. We learn the meaning of trusting in God because life can be unfair, filled with disappointments and overflowing with grief. The Scriptures tell us that we will have suffering on this earth and that it is common for every Christian to experience it. Peter writes to Christians in the first century, encouraging them to hold on to their faith in hard times:

> Keep your guard up. You're not the only ones plunged into these hard times. It's the same with Christians all over the world. So keep a firm grip on the faith. The suffering won't last forever. It won't be long before this generous God who has great plans for us in Christ—eternal and glorious plans they are!—will have you put together and on your feet for good. He gets the last word; yes, he does.
> (1 Peter 5:9-11, The Message)

How can we overcome like some of these heroes of faith in the

Bible? How did those early Christians do it in the face of death? How can we have genuine trust in God when it is beyond our own strength? Often, trusting God seems easier for everyone else. And though we may feel weak, God's power takes control in our lives, so that we can overcome through the difficulties. It is precisely when we are "not in control" that Jesus is actually "in control." His power exists now and forever. It is real. It is always available to us.

There was nothing that anyone could say to Chaz and Ginger or to Laura to take away their hurt as they went through their trials. There are no easy answers to pain such as this. God himself has endured the pain of losing a child, his only Son. His Son suffered at the hands of evil men. Even though Jesus only did good to people while on this earth, he was rejected, spat upon and crucified. Yet, he never gave up. He trusted in his Father in heaven, even as he faced the trials ahead of him. Remember, despite the great sacrifice and suffering, there was no guarantee that men and women would respond to his love.

3
LEARNING FROM JACOB

Let us look at a man in the Bible whose faith was shaped and defined by the struggles that he faced throughout his lifetime. His name was Jacob. He was later renamed "Israel" by the Lord, but that renaming came at a price—through hardships and trials. His life started with a father who did not love him very much, and with an older brother who despised him. Of course, Jacob was not innocent in all of this. He had been deceitful as a child towards his father and his brother. He was forced to learn a painful lesson about deception from his uncle Laban—Jacob had to work for his wife, Rachel, fourteen years then work an additional six years with his wages being changed ten times (Genesis 31:7, 38). In addition, all the men in

Jacob's life including his "father figures" were a disappointment to him. It was his faith and devotion to God that provided light and guidance in his life. In fact, he found a true and faithful father in God.

Let us start from the beginning of his life and watch how he grows in his relationship with his Father in heaven.

> When the boys grew up, Esau was a skillful hunter, a man of the field, while Jacob was a quiet man, dwelling in tents. Isaac loved Esau because he ate of his game; but Rebekah loved Jacob. (Genesis 25:27, RSV)

It does not say that Isaac did not love Jacob, but it is clear through this verse that he favored Esau over Jacob. Isaac appreciated the outdoor talents and abilities in his son Esau more than those of his son Jacob.

> When Isaac was old and his eyes were so weak that he could no longer see, he called for Esau his older son and said to him, "My son."
>
> "Here I am," he answered.
>
> Isaac said, "I am now an old man and don't know the day of my death. Now then, get your weapons—your quiver and bow—and go out to the open country to hunt some wild game for me. Prepare me the kind of tasty food I like and bring it to me to eat, so that I may give you my blessing before I die." (Genesis 27:1-4)

Rebekah, Isaac's wife, was listening to the conversation as Isaac spoke to Esau. She quickly approaches Jacob and convinces him to deceive his father so that he would receive the blessing reserved for Esau. Even though Jacob is afraid, he agrees to do as his mother asks. Many years later during the time of Moses, God commands that the firstborn receive a double portion by law (Deuteronomy 21:17).

Though God would have been pleased with Isaac blessing Esau as the older son, there were no blessings reserved for his second son at all. In fact, when Esau tries to recover some blessing from his father, there is nothing left for him to receive.

> Esau said, "Isn't he rightly named Jacob? He has deceived me these two times: He took my birthright, and now he's taken my blessing!" Then he asked, "Haven't you reserved any blessing for me?"
>
> Isaac answered Esau, "I have made him lord over you and have made all his relatives his servants, and I have sustained him with grain and new wine. So what can I possibly do for you, my son?"
>
> Esau said to his father, "Do you have only one blessing, my father? Bless me too, my father!" Then Esau wept aloud.
>
> His father Isaac answered him,
>
> "Your dwelling will be
>   away from the earth's richness,
>   away from the dew of heaven above.
> You will live by the sword
>   and you will serve your brother.
> But when you grow restless,
>   you will throw his yoke
>   from off your neck." (Genesis 27:36-40)

It was truly a sad day for Esau. He was left in torment, knowing that there was not even one blessing left for him. It must have been equally a shock for Jacob to realize that his father had not intended to bless Jacob at all before his death! Every blessing given by Isaac had been intended for only his eldest son, Esau. Although he ended up with all the blessings, Jacob was not favored by his father and was hated by his brother. His deception revealed a painful truth about his family, and it eventually took him away from his home, his mother and his relationships, leaving him a lonely man.

In all of this, however, God had a bigger plan which allowed Jacob to begin a new chapter in his life. The next period of long and difficult years was crucial for him in finding God and building a deep relationship with him. Without these events, Jacob would have not experienced the revelation from God on his journey.

4
GOD'S PURPOSES IN HIS GUIDANCE

Some of us have come from homes in which there was very little or no love. The relationships inside the family did not offer security but rather insecurity and fear. Home was not as sweet for us as we might have desired it to be. In fact, we could not wait to leave home when we finally got into college or got our first job.

For others of us, even if there was love in our homes, there were also ever-present problems—perhaps never so terrible that we would run away, but enough to leave scars in our hearts.

Then, there are also among us, the blessed few, who have grown up in faithful Christian families.

No matter our background or experience, all of these factors in our lives opened our hearts to a path that led us to our Lord Jesus Christ.

For Jacob, the rejection he faced from his father and brother after deceiving them became the impetus for him to leave home. It allowed God to begin working in his life so that Jacob would turn to him. No longer under his mother's control. No longer competing with his older twin brother. No longer feeling worthless in his father's sight. No longer under the influence of his family, Jacob was now on his own to make his own choices for his life and find God, who was his protector and provider. His journey to finding the light of God begins with a dream that changed the direction of his life forever.

> He had a dream in which he saw a stairway resting on the earth, with its top reaching to heaven, and the angels of God were ascending and descending on it. There above it stood the LORD, and he said, "I am the LORD, the God of your father Abraham and the God of Isaac. I will give you and your descendants the land on which you are lying. Your descendants will be like the dust of the earth, and you will spread out to the west and to the east, to the north and to the south. All peoples on earth will be blessed through you and your offspring. I am with you and will watch over you wherever you go, and I will bring you back to this land. I will not leave you until I have done what I have promised you." (Genesis 28:12-15)

Jacob leaves Beersheba and sets out for Haran—a four-hundred-mile journey on foot, which is about twenty days, nearly a month, to visit his uncle Laban. He has no money, no food and no belongings with him except the bare minimum necessary for such a long journey. This new phase was the beginning of his walk with God. His dream gave him hope and opened his eyes to the God of his fathers.

God had made some incredible promises to him—a new land, many descendants, blessings and guidance as well as the promise of bringing him home someday. With this dream and these promises from God, Jacob makes a pledge to God, to make him his Lord if God fulfills his promises (Genesis 28:20–22). This turning point, however, did not guarantee him a perfect life as we will see later.

Jacob was walking in the dark, hoping to touch the white fence, not seeing what lay ahead of him. All he had were God's promises to stand on. We see in Jacob's life that he grew closer to his God through the experiences in his life. He matured through every difficulty rather than deteriorate in bitterness and anger. He became a better man who overcame victoriously, and his life became the seed for the nation of Israel. The struggle and fight earned him the right to be a father of faith.

In the same way, God knows our hearts and intends our challenges to be a part of a spiritual journey in our lives. Parts of the journey can be dark; we can feel hopeless because we cannot see ahead of us. Let's keep our hands held out, reaching, because we know that we will be touching the fence soon. It's there. God has great purposes for our lives no matter who we are. We may not become a great nation, but maybe an incredible mother. We may not inherit a promised land, but hopefully inherit a faith that will be passed down through generations. We may be on a road to becoming something that we would have never imagined before.

5

OPPORTUNITIES THROUGH CHALLENGES

God was not finished with Jacob even after his fourteen years with Laban. God was going to allow Jacob to confront one of his greatest fears: his brother, Esau. God would give Jacob the opportunity to be reunited with his brother as well as to face his fears. Because of the great distance between Haran and Beersheba, Jacob had remained very separate from that part of his life. In fact, it was easy for him to ignore the issue and pretend it did not exist.

God sets the time and place for all of us to confront our fears and our problems. There may be a situation in your life that you have effectively avoided for months and even years. God knows when you are ready to handle dealing with those people or those circumstances. He will arrange for you to finally confront that relationship or that situation. Most likely, he will make it unavoidable. God loves you too much to allow you to run away from unresolved issues. He will set in motion the events to make you deal with your life, no matter how long it takes.

After fourteen years, God set the stage for Jacob to finally face his brother. He left his uncle, Laban, and took his family with him to go back home. Angels meet him on the way to encourage him (Genesis 32:1).

Then, a messenger comes to tell Jacob that his brother is headed his way with four hundred men! This was an unforeseen problem. He was already afraid of his brother since he was bigger and stronger than he. And, now, he was coming toward him with an army (Genesis 32:6–11). He also knew that he had wronged Esau greatly. Jacob had tricked his brother and hurt him so much that it was understandable that Esau would want to kill him.

Jacob had not forgotten Esau's threat before leaving his homeland. He had no idea what Esau had in mind to do to him; so with Esau approaching him with four hundred men, he could only assume that Esau was still angry with him and was going to kill him. His fear drove him to his knees before the throne of his God. He wrestled all night with the Lord, struggling so much that his hip socket was wrenched out. It was not only a spiritual battle for him but also a physical one as he fought all night. Some say that this was Jacob's great effort in prayer. Others say that it was a true wrestling bout with the Lord (Genesis 32:24–30). Even as he exerted himself, Jacob remembered God's promise to make him prosper and to make his descendants like the sand on the seashore (Genesis 32:12).

6

Remembering the Cross of Christ

It is often during the midst of our hardest struggles that we remember our Lord. In fact, we finally turn to God after we have exhausted all our resources and relationships and find that we have nowhere else to turn. Before going to the cross, Jesus pleaded with God all night just as Jacob struggled with God until sunrise. Jesus was under such intense anguish that Luke reports that he *sweat* drops of blood (22:44). Many great men and women of God have faced their suffering and fought to gain strength from God. Even Jesus went before the throne of God and begged the other disciples to do the same on his behalf.

On September 15, 1995, I received a distressing phone call. I had been out all morning. When I returned home, there were several messages on my phone. The messages were all from different relatives urging me to call home as soon as possible. I even got a call from my brother's parents-in-law, which was extremely unusual. Through a series of phone calls, I was finally able to contact my father at work. He seemed in so much anguish that he could not even talk to me. A long time friend of the family, who was working for my father, took the phone from him and spoke to me instead. Confusion, agony and tears came crashing down on me as she informed me of my little brother's sudden death. He had been in a serious car wreck, and it killed him instantly. He was only thirty years old, married and had a three-year-old little boy named Hiroaki.

My brother was my best friend growing up. I wept loudly from the moment I heard the news all the way into the following morning, even when there were no more tears left to shed. I knelt by my sofa in the living room and remained there for hours, soaking the cushions with my tears. I did not sleep the entire night.

Grief was a familiar visitor in my life. Yet, I would have never suspected my little brother to be the one leaving this world at such a young age. Disbelief and shock clouded my heart as I reached out to the Lord in prayer. I could not imagine what my sister-in-law was going through at that moment. More than that, I did not know how a three-year-old boy could understand such a sudden tragedy.

My husband, Frank, sat by me all night and did not say a word.

He just held me in his arms as I wept. We got on a plane that next morning and flew from Tokyo to New York. Nothing that anyone said or did seemed to alleviate any of the pain that I felt in my heart. Those weeks and months that followed were a blur of anguish. At the same time, there was an unexplainable strength that came over me after that night of agonizing tears and prayer. It gave me the power to pour out my heart to my sister-in-law and love her through that time.

After Jacob's night of prayer or wrestling match with the Lord, his name was changed from "deceiver" to "Israel," which means "he struggles with God" (Genesis 32:28). Jacob's name was not the only aspect of his life that was altered. His relationship with God became the source of his strength, thus making him the father of the nation of Israel. It was his struggle with God that gave Jacob a mature and transformed relationship with God. He learned to be victorious over his struggles. Jacob was not going to give up that night before his encounter with Esau. He was intent on being victorious. He was going to conquer his fears and face them with God.

As I mentioned, in the same way, Jesus also wrestled in prayer all night before going to the cross.

> During the days of Jesus' life on earth, he offered up prayers and petitions with loud cries and tears to the one who could save him from death, and he was heard because of his reverent submission. Although he was a son, he learned obedience from what he suffered and, once made perfect, he became the source of eternal salvation for all who obey him and was designated by God to be high priest in the order of Melchizedek. (Hebrews 5:7-10)

Jesus became a real human being. He had to go through suffering like any other person to become "perfect," so that he could die for our sins. Though he was already perfect as the sinless Son of

God, the fact that he suffered made him the perfect redeemer for mankind. Suffering is what usually drives an individual to sin: cheat, steal, lie, hate, kill, slander, etc. But Jesus learned obedience from what he had suffered, making him worthy to become a high priest in the order of Melchizedek. The only fact known about this high priest, Melchizedek, is that he was king of Salem and priest of God Most High (Hebrews 7:1–3). His name meant "king of righteousness" as well as "king of Salem." When Abraham returned from the defeat of the kings, this priest blessed him.

Dark and fearful times bring us to our knees—even the Son of God was not an exception. All the heroes in the Bible went to God when there was only darkness—no light within sight. Those are the times when we are carried on God's loving arms through our prayers and the prayers of others. We do not see the answers right away, but often we discover how valuable our relationship with God is.

Our light should never become a nicer home, a better job, a promotion or success. None of these gains will enable us to see the throne of God more clearly. It is when we are able to face our weaknesses through the darkness and turn to see the light of God that we will achieve true victory and attain a reward. We will never change our shortcomings in an instant nor will we get rid of all our hardships. But we can learn to depend on God through our struggles. Then he will become our light as we trust and rely on him. And in the end, God will do the rest.

Amidst those bleak times, our faith gets stretched to its very limits. But God shines his light powerfully in the darkness. In fact, the darker it becomes, the brighter the light shines. Satan will tempt us to give up, to mistrust and to become angry at God. He will push us so hard that we will even be tempted to renounce our faith. We, however, need to remember that in overcoming through these despairing times, not only are our names changed, but ourselves as well—we are transformed into the likeness of Christ. And our names will be written in heaven!

I am thankful that amidst the darkness of my brother's death, God allowed me to see the light. His hope, his guidance, his love and his mercy were a lamp in the obscurity. At just the right moment, God lit his lamp for me so that I could go running to him. As a result of this tragedy, my sister-in-law became a Christian and is remarried to a wonderful Christian man who loves her very much. My nephew, Hiroaki, is now a teenager, and a faithful Christian. He has a new sister and brother whom he loves with all his heart. God is truly an amazing God!

God's strength will become our strength when we reach out to him in prayer and struggle to overcome. He is always there to listen even in the darkest of times. God allows us to walk toward "that fence" in the darkness, but he is ready and waiting, prepared to illuminate his lamp. Let us open our eyes to Jesus and see the path of light that he has set before us as we walk with him through the best and the worst of times and watch him work his miracles.

Let us all make Jesus our light and follow its radiance so that he can meet us at the end of the course.

STUDY QUESTIONS

Spiritual Light: How Can I See When It's So Dark?

1. In this chapter, we saw how Jesus can light the path during the tough times in our lives. Even when we see little or no hope, Jesus can help us to see purpose and direction in those dark times.

   a. What kind of challenges are you facing right now in your life? How are you dealing with your fears and anxieties during this time?

   b. How are you allowing this time to shape your faith and life?

Are you letting Jesus take the lead?

   c. Have you been praying through your situation? What are you learning through your challenges?

2. How have tragedies, hardships and challenges shaped your life in the past? As you look back, in what ways do you realize you have been transformed by them?

3. Jesus is the light in times of darkness. How have you been able to see the light through divorce, death, unemployment, broken relationships, or other difficult times?

4. What are you afraid to face in your life right now? Are you ready to face it with God?

5. Make a decision to take one situation that you have been avoiding and start praying daily about it. Allow God to work in your heart so that one day you can deal with it once and for all.

2

Satan

DOES HE HAVE POWER OVER ME?

> The devil has been sinning since the beginning, so anyone
> who continues to sin belongs to the devil. The Son of God
> came for this purpose: to destroy the devil's work.
>
> 1 John 3:8 (NCV)

1
WHO HAS THE POWER IN THIS WORLD?

Now, I want to invite you to open your heart as we explore the characteristics of Satan. Despite the fact that Satan is mentioned various times throughout the Scriptures, his existence and his power are often overlooked among Christians. Taking many forms, he is a dominant force in this world. Understanding his characteristics will help us to be aware of his schemes and his intentions. Because he is real, he cannot be ignored as a part of the reality in our world today. His wickedness and evil are prevalent all around us. In our everyday lives, Satan is working to thwart all of God's plans. More than that, his lies and his trickery are poisonous to our souls.

According to the Scriptures, Satan has many names. Jesus calls him "the prince of this world" (John 12:31, 14:30, 16:11). Paul calls him "the god of this age" (2 Corinthians 4:4). He is also called "the serpent" (Genesis 3:1, 2 Corinthians 11:3, Revelation 12:9, 20:2). He "masquerades as an angel of light" (2 Corinthians 11:14). He is also known as "the angel of the Abyss," who is named Abaddon or Apollyon, both translated as "the destroyer" (Revelation 9:11) because he tries to destroy our souls. Sometimes his schemes are very subtle. Other times, his tactics are aggressive as he desires to tear down everything good.

When we give in to Satan and allow him to control our minds and our actions, we do not feel or see his evil as clearly. This is why we need to be constantly on the alert. He is "the father of lies and a murderer" (John 8:44).

Satan is best known as the devil and sometimes as Lucifer (KJV). He has dominion over this world and controls many people. Jesus refers to Satan as the prince of this world because God allows Satan to have power and authority in this world. His influence, however, is not obvious to us unless we are aware of his schemes. The stronger we try to fight against him, the fiercer his power becomes against us.

Satan wants to ruin righteous men and women. It says in the Scriptures that Job was blameless and upright (Job 1:1). Obviously, this did not please Satan at all. He wanted to destroy Job's integrity and make him even curse God! How many of us can be written up in the Bible by God as being blameless and upright? What an incredible challenge to even be considered by God to have any of the attributes that Job did!

> One day the angels came to present themselves before the LORD, and Satan also came with them. The LORD said to Satan, "Where have you come from?"
>
> Satan answered the LORD, "From roaming through the earth and going back and forth in it."
>
> Then the LORD said to Satan, "Have you considered my servant Job? There is no one on earth like him; he is blameless and upright, a man who fears God and shuns evil."
>
> "Does Job fear God for nothing," Satan replied. "Have

you not put a hedge around him and his household and
everything he has? You have blessed the work of his
hands, so that his flocks and herds are spread throughout
the land. But stretch out your hand and strike everything he
has, and he will surely curse you to your face."
(Job 1:6-11)

Satan is an accuser—he indicts God and his people. Satan
believed that Job was upright only because God protected him and
allowed him to flourish. He was confident that he could easily anni-
hilate the honor and purity of Job. When given the opportunity,
Satan would show no mercy to Job. Accordingly, calamity struck at
every corner of Job's home and family. Aggressively and mercilessly,
Satan destroyed everything he owned and loved. Let us look at Job's
response after experiencing such disaster.

At this, Job got up and tore his robe and shaved his
head. Then he fell to the ground in worship and said:
"Naked I came from my mother's womb,
and naked I will depart.
The LORD gave and the LORD has taken away;
may the name of the LORD be praised."

In all this, Job did not sin by charging God with wrongdoing. (Job 1:20-22)

Job did not sin. Instead, he tore his robe and worshiped the
Lord. How many of us would respond like Job in the face of such
calamity and sorrow? Satan wanted to make Job sin. He wanted to
devastate Job's life and faith. He was willing to do anything to
accomplish this. No matter how hard he struck, Job relied on his
relationship with God in increasing measure. Regardless of how persistent Satan was, Job did not give in.

Job was not an easy target as he remained steadfast through

Satan's onslaughts. God knew Job's heart and was convinced of his righteousness. God knew that Job could overcome the challenges of Satan because of his faithfulness. God was aware of Job's heart because he sees the hearts of men (1 Samuel 16:7). In the same way, God always knows our limitations and will never allow hardships and challenges to push us beyond our ability to endure (1 Corinthians 10:13).

For Job, the attacks of Satan did not end with the destruction of his home and the deaths of his sons and daughters. Satan was, once again, bored in his wanderings on the earth (Job 2:1–9). This time, his attacks on Job are even fiercer, giving Job painful sores all over his body. At this point, his wife tells Job to curse God. She was bitter in her soul and tried to convince Job to sin. In this, Satan uses his wife to tempt him to reject God.

Job was honest with God about his thoughts. At times, he spoke back to God and to the men who rebuked him. He even challenged God and asked to understand why these things were happening when he had been faithful to God. In his hurt and his honesty, he went to God for answers. He showed his faith and integrity in staying in dialogue with God. Though he was not perfect in all his ways, he never let go of his relationship with God.

God reminded Job who he (God) was—his power, his supremacy, his might. With a humble heart, Job realized that he had questioned God, and he repented. His integrity of heart as he wrestled with difficult situations ended up being affirmed and blessed by God. He passed the test that Satan had brought to him.

He did not end up blaming God for his difficulties and did not become bitter despite the catastrophe that had struck him. Instead, he drew closer to God, relying on him with all his heart.

Just as he attacked Job, Satan will attack God's people over and over again. He might relent for a while, but he will return with a different scheme to try to make us fall. His craftiness tries to twist the goodness in people. The accuser only blames. He does not look at himself. He does not see all the wickedness within his existence. He looks at what is good and defines it as evil in one form or another. Satan confounds the light and makes it appear as darkness—that is his role and his strategy. He criticizes any characteristic that may be godly and pure.

Satan has no concern for people. He wants to conquer the virtuous and make them his slaves by turning them against God. He stands especially close to those who are persistent in doing God's will. He launches emotional attacks such as hurting our family. He unleashes physical problems—illness, an accident or surgery. He instigates troubles in our marriage or our friendships. He manipulates us with failure and weakness. Those over whom he triumphs often become deceived and convinced of his lies (1 Timothy 4:1, Titus 1:15–16, 2 Peter 2:1–3).

On the other hand, the devil cannot be victorious against faith. Though he will be merciless at times, stand firm, dear sisters. The King of kings and the Lord of lords has already overcome this evil prince (John 16:11, 33). The prince of this world has no power over us as long as we hold to the power of heaven and not to the powers of this world. God will deliver us as long as we pray and rely on him (Matthew 6:13, 2 Corinthians 1:10, 1 John 4:4).

2

How Did Satan Come About?

In Revelation 12, the apostle John describes a war in heaven (Revelation 12:7–9). We do not know much about this battle except that Satan was once an angel in heaven. We are not told why or how he changed from being good to being evil. Over time, he became prideful and arrogant, to the point that he was convinced of his ability to overcome God. He even persuaded some of the other angels to join him in his war against God and his angels. His rebellion cost him his place in heaven and, as a result, that great dragon—Satan—was hurled to the earth.

According to Scripture, Satan was not sent to hell. Often, people think that Satan's home is in hell or down below the earth. Contrary to this popular belief, the Bible states very clearly in this passage of Scripture that Satan's home is in this world—the earth. His home is where all of us live! No wonder this world can seem like "hell" especially as we read the newspapers and watch television about wars, murders, rape and embezzlement happening daily around the world. All the wickedness and evil in our society does not originate with God but with the evil one.

Previously, we saw in the book of Job that Satan was just "hanging out" on the earth looking for his next victim.

> And the LORD said unto Satan, "Whence comest thou?"
> Then Satan answered the Lord, and said, "From going to
> and fro in the earth, and from walking up and down in it."
> (Job 1:7, KJV)

From the beginning of time, Satan was on the earth, ready to oppose whenever God did something good—whether it was the creation in the Garden of Eden or on the cross of Jesus for the salvation of the world. Satan has always been persistent in carrying out his wicked plans. In fact, the devil wanted to destroy the most beloved of God's creation—man.

Imagine the joy that God had when he created man and woman. They were the pinnacle of his creation. He blessed them and commanded them to be fruitful and multiply. Everything that God created was good (Genesis 1:31). Human beings and angels were never meant to be evil but were given a choice. Satan, the ancient serpent, chose to be evil. He chose to fight against God and to become his eternal enemy. But God will someday condemn Satan forever.

3

SATAN'S WEAPONS FOR MASS DESTRUCTION

> Now the serpent was more crafty than any of the wild
> animals the LORD God had made. He said to the woman,
> "Did God really say, 'You must not eat from any tree in the
> garden'?"
> The woman said to the serpent, "We may eat fruit from
> the trees in the garden, but God did say, 'You must not eat
> fruit from the tree that is in the middle of the garden, and
> you must not touch it, or you will die.'"
> "You will not surely die," the serpent said to the woman.
> (Genesis 3:1–4)

Satan is so crafty that he takes the form of one of the wild animals in the garden and speaks to Eve. During their brief conversation, the serpent puts doubts in the woman's mind by twisting and
contradicting God's word. Satan is bold. He repeats what God has
said to her, with a slight twist: "Did God really say, 'You must not eat
fruit from any tree in the garden'?" Eve understood what God had
said. She knew that it was only the one tree in the middle of the garden which was not meant to be touched. Yet, Satan cunningly dis-
torts then challenges what God says by telling Eve that she would
not die from eating the forbidden fruit. Here are God's actual words:

> And the LORD God commanded the man, "You are free to
> eat from *any tree* in the garden; but you must not eat from
> the tree of the knowledge of good and evil, for when you
> eat of it you will surely die." (Genesis 2:16–17, emphasis
> added).

God had told Adam and Eve that they were free to eat from *any*
tree in the garden except from the *one* tree in the middle of the garden. Satan twists God's words in order to make God look bad.

Furthermore, Satan makes Eve feel like God had placed many limitations on her when there was only one restriction.

Isn't this the way Satan gets us to doubt God? Satan tries to convince us that God has set numerous limitations in our lives, keeping us from having any "fun" or "freedom." The commands we struggle with get blown out of proportion in our minds. In fact, we feel like we cannot be a "good" Christian because of that "one" command from God. We focus on the negatives and not the positives of what God wants for our lives. God wanted Adam and Eve to have an abundant life in the Garden of Eden where they would be able to have all their needs met. Instead, they forfeited all of it, because they believed Satan rather than God.

Believe it or not, slavery and lack of freedom actually come from Satan (John 8:34–36)! He enslaves us to all our earthly desires. After a while, we feel like we cannot live without the fleshly desires of our hearts. They entrap us and make us disobedient to God and his word. This is exactly how Satan worked in ensnaring Eve in the Garden of Eden.

> When the woman saw that the fruit of the tree was good for food and pleasing to the eye, and also desirable for gaining wisdom, she took some and ate it. She also gave some to her husband, who was with her, and he ate it. (Genesis 3:6)

Eve got too close to the one tree that she was not supposed to eat from. Probably, she was intrigued by the fact that it was forbidden and went right up to the tree to see what made it so "special." This gave Satan, the serpent, the opportunity to attack Eve with his lies and deception. Let us look closely at this verse to see how Satan influenced Eve to fall into temptation and disobey God.

First, Eve reasoned that the fruit from the tree was "good for food." Second, it was "pleasing to the eye." Third, it was "desirable for gaining wisdom." Interestingly enough, the apostle John warns us of these exact temptations from the world. Let us look at the following scripture from 1 John.

> Do not love the world or anything in the world. If anyone loves the world, the love of the Father is not in him. For everything in the world—the cravings of sinful man *(good for food)*, the lust of his eyes *(pleasing to the eye)* and the boasting of what he has and does *(desirable for gaining wisdom)*—comes not from the Father but from the world. The world and its desires pass away, but the man who does the will of God lives forever. (1 John 2:15-17, italicized parenthetical phrases added)

What are the temptations in your life right now? What is luring you to sin? Have you been overcoming your struggles? The problems in our lives do not come from our wanting to love the world. In fact, most of us women try to steer away from worldliness. But then we go to school and see a friend with the latest outfit on and feel a tinge of envy—and in our hearts we say, *That's too expensive for me to afford, but boy, do I want that. And, yuk, her outfit makes her look so shapely!*

Or we go to the mall, past the Coach store, past Brendan Jewelers, past the iPod Store, and our eyes get averted from the goal. Just a tiny peek inside. Just a quick trip into the changing room. Just a little look at those pretty things. And, we end up buying something that we didn't really need.

Women are stimulated visually as much or more than men. If you look at the magazine racks, almost all the women's magazines are filled with mostly pictures and very few words. We love looking at clothes, homes, beautiful gardens and delicious food! Think about it: what man do you know who loves receiving flowers? But when a woman gets a bouquet of roses, she is overjoyed, flaunting them to her friends, sniffing them every time she looks at them. Most men do not react in the same way. We women find joy in such beauty and fragrances. It is our strength and our weakness at the same time. This is how we fall into Satan's trap.

Eve saw the fruit—it looked delicious. The fragrance was over-powering—she needed to get a better whiff of its aroma. So Eve went closer and closer to the forbidden tree until she was within reach of the fruit. And, boy did those pieces of fruit look beautiful—better than the fruit from the other trees around her! The tree of life was right next to it, but the fruit on the forbidden tree looked better.

As she turned away to look at the tree of life again, the serpent somehow got her attention to look the other way. He spoke to her, tempted her and initiated her fall. But he didn't stop there; he used her to influence Adam to fall as well.

Somewhere inside of us, we convince ourselves that we need what we don't have. The fruit on the forbidden tree looks attractive, and we want to look attractive to hide those bulges and bumps that should not be there, but are. That is where the "cravings of sinful man" come from—which then becomes "the lust of the eye." We look for ways to hide what we do not like about ourselves: our body, our house, our car and other aspects of our lives. We rationalize the benefits and become entrapped by the thoughts of "boasting of what [we have] and [do]."

Even Jesus was tempted through these same three steps during his forty-day fast. He needed food to survive, yes, but he was fasting. In the desert while Jesus fasted, the first of the series of Satan's temptations was "the cravings of sinful man." Just as Eve thought that the forbidden fruit was good for food, Jesus was tempted by Satan to turn a rock into bread, a strong desire, especially after fasting for many days (Luke 4:3).

Next, Satan leads Jesus to a high place and allures him with the riches of the world.

> The devil led him up to a high place and showed him in an instant all the kingdoms of the world. And he said to him, "I will give you all their authority and splendor, for it has been given to me, and I can give it to anyone I want to. So if you worship me, it will all be yours." (Luke 4:5-7)

In the above scripture, Satan uses the splendor of the world to try to entrap Jesus. Satan's scheme of appealing to the "lust of his eyes" (1 John 2:16) is evident here. Just like the fruit in the Garden of Eden, the treasures of the world are appealing to the eye. It was a real temptation for Jesus. We can know this because he was tempted just as we are (Hebrews 4:15). And isn't this a temptation for each one of us? This is how television and commercials entice us. They convince us that our lives would be better if we owned a nicer car, a bigger house or more stylish clothes. Our eyes can draw us into a world of greed and materialism. Satan knows our hearts and our weakness in these areas.

The final lure of Satan during Jesus' forty-day fast related to the "boasting of what he has and does" (1 John 2:16). Let us look at the scripture below to understand this temptation more clearly.

> For the third test the Devil took him to Jerusalem and put him on top of the Temple. He said, "If you are God's Son, jump. It's written, isn't it, that 'he placed you in the care of angels to protect you; they will catch you; you won't so much as stub you toe on a stone'?"
>
> "Yes," said Jesus, "and it's also written, 'Don't you dare tempt the Lord your God'."
>
> That completed the testing. The Devil retreated temporarily, lying in wait for another opportunity. (Luke 4:9-13, The Message)

Satan tries to convince Jesus through the Scriptures that he had power to command God's angels, in this way enticing Jesus to "boast of what he has and does" (1 John 2:16). In the same way, Eve was tempted by her pride to gain knowledge. Jesus was tempted by pride to prove his powers and to even test God with them.

Satan, however, fails in all three of his attempts with Jesus, finally leaving him alone. Meanwhile, Satan waits patiently for a more opportune time (Luke 4:13).

Sadly, it only took one try with Adam and Eve to get them to sin. The result was that they were banished from the Garden of Eden forever.

We can also become deceived like Adam and Eve. If, however, we are aware of the devil's schemes, we can fight back effectively just as Jesus did. Satan is very predictable in his areas of temptation. When we understand how he strikes, we can deal with our spiritual lives more wisely.

Many of us remain baffled about Satan and his power over us even though the Scriptures make his evil ways clear. Let us remember that Satan cannot control us as long as we rely on God's word. Open your eyes to his ways, and you will be able to overcome his temptations and evil schemes. Consider the following scripture shared earlier.

> Keep a cool head. Stay alert. The Devil is poised to pounce, and would like nothing better than to catch you napping. Keep your guard up. You're not the only ones plunged into these hard times. It's the same with Christians all over the world. So keep a firm grip on the faith. The suffering won't last forever. It won't be long before this generous God who has great plans for us in Christ—eternal and glorious plans they are!—will have you put together and on your feet for good. He gets the last word; yes, he does. (1 Peter 5:8 – 11, The Message)

4

RECOGNIZING SATAN'S LIES

Have you ever been tricked? Have people ever deceived you into thinking a certain way and later on you realized that it was all a lie? Have you ever stretched the truth to someone you loved in order "not to hurt them"? These are questions that hit at the core of a Christian's heart as we battle with our personal honesty and truthfulness. We look at the lies of other people with disdain while our own half-truths and falsehoods have a "sensible" excuse and reason. In this way, lies can deceive the deceiver. Whether they are "white lies" or obvious deception, God sees no light in the darkness. How about us? What do we see?

My husband is a fun-loving man. He used to love to tease and to play tricks on me. I say "used to" because after over twenty-four years of marriage, I have him figured out. For this reason, he has given up trying. There were many humorous moments in the early years of our marriage as Frank tried extremely hard to make me laugh or have fun by playing pranks on me.

During the first year of our marriage, we lived in an unsafe section of Boston. For this reason, as a habit before going to bed, Frank would go through the house to lock all the doors and windows that had been left open during the day. One night, while he was locking the doors and windows, he decided to pretend that an intruder had come into the house. He made banging noises as well as grunting sounds of a fist fight that reverberated into our bedroom, where I nervously waited for him. He knocked down chairs and banged on the doors causing quite a commotion in the living room.

Being the naïve newlywed that I was, I became frightened and called out for him from the bedroom. When only silence followed, I ventured out into the living room thinking that he might just be fooling around. In the meantime, Frank was smiling in the corner of the dark room waiting for me. I walked right into his trap as I stepped into the living room! There, from the recesses of the dark room, he jumped out at me and shouted out a big "Boo!" My sneaky husband scared me so much that it took me a few moments before I could laugh with him.

There were many other instances of this type during the first few years of our marriage. We often laugh about those funny stories. As time went by, however, it became more challenging for him to trick me. He finally stopped all his crazy efforts after one bad experience. It was the classic "The Boy Who Cried Wolf" event that made Frank think twice before trying to fool me again.

It happened on one sunny morning, very early. As soon as the alarm went off, he jumped out of bed, ready for the morning. I was going to stay in bed for a few more minutes until the morning "grogginess" wore off. Suddenly, I heard loud banging sounds in the hallway. I couldn't believe that he was starting so early in the morning with his practical jokes! Routinely, I shouted out to see if he was all right. And as usual, there was no response. I even cried out from the bedroom, "I'm not going out there so you can scare me!"

For several minutes there was absolute silence, so I got up from my bed and headed into the hallway. This time, Frank was lying face down on the ground. I started to laugh and told him that it was too early in the morning for his hoaxes. Even with my warnings, he lay still. At this point, I still believed that he was fooling around and turned him over onto his back. There was blood dripping down his face! Believe it or not, I thought that he had put ketchup on his face!

As I was preoccupied by the thought of how he got the ketchup on his face so quickly, he regained consciousness. It took me a few moments to realize that my husband had really passed out and hurt himself this time. He had fainted from getting up too quickly, and then he knocked himself out by hitting the corner of the door thus cutting his forehead open with a big wound.

Needless to say, our whole morning turned into one long visit to the emergency room. Frank ended up with five stitches on his forehead for his injury! We laughed as we went home from the hospital. I gave him a new name—"Frankenstein"—since his sutured forehead was similar to the one from the movie character.

That incident caused Frank to retire from his pranks. We were reminded of the dangers of playing practical jokes, even seemingly harmless ones. I also learned to be more alert so that I could differentiate between an accident and a practical joke. In fact, I cannot remember the last time he tried to trick me after that event. It could have been more serious, but we were young and did not think about the possible price of our "fun."

Though joking around can be amusing, Satan's schemes are not comical. His tricks are real and have serious consequences. This makes it even more crucial for us to be able to distinguish between truth and lies—the light from the darkness—reality from deceit—and righteousness from falsehood. If we make ourselves more aware of Satan's methods of deception, we will be able to see through his mendacity, or dishonesty, and we will overcome the world (1 John 4:1; 5:4–5).

5
PREVENTING OURSELVES FROM BEING DECEIVED

In a world so full of lies, how can we see the truth? How can we keep ourselves from being deceived? What can help us to be more aware of such deception? How can we stand firm in our faith amidst all the dishonesty around us?

Often, we try to make a distinction between the good and the bad by taking a negative approach. That is, instead of seeking the truth, we look for deceitfulness in others. God always blesses the seeker of truth by granting them wisdom because a man or a woman seeking truth will learn to discern the lies from the truth.

> The heart of the discerning acquires knowledge,
>   the ears of the wise seek it out. (Proverbs 18:15)

It is a part of human nature to focus on the negative aspects of life rather than the positives. Look at the news on TV; there is rarely any good news reported. In fact, it is a known fact that newspapers reporting a lot of good news do not sell. People want to hear the latest gossip, shocking events and horrific tragedies because these are more exciting. In the same way, seeking out truth can sound boring for the average person, whereas looking for scams, cheats and frauds is much more thrilling. Many movies and dramas are based on the theme of the main character searching for the lies in seemingly good people, and finding layers and layers of deception.

The desire to seek only the truth becomes increasingly difficult after having experienced hurts or betrayals in our lives. As we grow older, we encounter them to a greater and greater extent, making us more wary and distrusting of others. Consequently, many of us question God rather than grow closer to him through these difficulties. We ask questions such as; "Why did God let this happen to me even though I never hurt anyone?" or "If God is a loving God, why did he create a world with so much pain and suffering?"

Inside the cloud of doubts and questions, we ignore God's perspective of the world. God has no intention of hurting us or being cruel to us. Moreover, he loves us and has paid a hefty price to forgive us of our sins (1 John 4:10). This world is not his kingdom as we have seen earlier in this book. The sins and the evils of this world do not belong to God but to the father of lies, Satan (John 8:44). Knowing all of this, how can we maintain a perspective consistent with the truth?

Doubt causes fear. As women, we can be controlled by fear—even the fear of finding out the truth. We have had truth hurt us just as much as the lies. The consequences of hearing the truth have left some women feeling that it was better not to know it. Truths such as the answers to the following questions: *Is my father getting drunk, and is he going to beat my mom again tonight? Is my husband on the Internet looking at bad stuff again while I'm asleep? Do I really have cancer after all? Will we lose the house because of our debts?* When we are faced with questions such as these, sometimes we would rather not hear the truth. Instead we might prefer to ignore it—and hope that the whole situation will go away. We must first understand that finding the truth will also be the first step in finding solutions and getting help.

The devil's greatest enemy is Jesus. Jesus is defined by truth. The Bible says that he is full of grace and truth (John 1:14). Jesus' life and teachings are the antithesis of Satan and his ways.

Other heroes in the Bible fought for the truth and even died for it. Great men and women of faith such as Elijah, Elisha, Rahab, Hannah and Daniel, all sought God and his truth in a time when truth was not only difficult to find but had costly consequences. Just like these men and women of faith, we must choose to seek the truth and love it.

Let us not be afraid of the truth. God is calling each of us to reach a new level in our relationship with him. The devil is the one who does not want us to seek the truth. Jesus loves the truth, and so must we. Seeking the truth, however, doesn't mean that we will find the answers to all the "whys" of life. Searching for the truth will simply help us to see the world from God's broad and extensive point of view rather than from our limited and narrow viewpoint. In understanding the truth, we will be able to recognize God's plans and God's ways. Though we may never see all of the truths of life, we can be more equipped to handle Satan's attacks on our faith.

6

Pay the Price for Truth

Buy the truth and do not sell it;
   get wisdom, discipline and understanding.
(Proverbs 23:23)

Truth has a price. When we look for God's truth or desire to uncover the truth, it is no easy matter. Fortunately, God gives us a way to recognize it. His word gives us the wisdom to identify truth. Sometimes, however, it takes sacrifice and perseverance to take hold of this treasure. This is where many of us give up. When we are not willing to make the effort, it can prevent us from taking hold of God's wisdom. We, then, become trapped by Satan's deception and are prevented from seeing the entirety of God's reality.

On Monday, March 20, 1995, in Tokyo, one of the safest industrial capitols of the world, an unknown man left a bag containing deadly poison called sarin gas inside one of the subway cars as he disembarked. There was a timer inside the bag that was set to go off just a few seconds after he left the station. Within minutes, the train and subterranean station were filled with poisonous gas.

People groped around while suffocating from the horrible effects of the gas. Many simply passed out and died as they struggled for the exits to the subway station. Others choked and foamed at the mouth. The fumes of the deadly sarin gas spread throughout one of the busiest subway stations in Tokyo where millions take the train every day. Those who survived suffered permanent brain-damage while others who did not breathe in as much of the toxin were emotionally scarred from this incident.

As investigations sought out the truth about this heinous crime, it became clear that a Buddhist cult was responsible not only for this event but several other unsolved murders in Japan. The mastermind behind these evil operations was a leader named Asahara Shoko. The detectives discovered that all the people who tried to expose his plots had secretly been disposed of one by one. Their bodies were never found, and their disappearance remains a mystery to this day. Many men and women joined this cult and believed their evil teachings. Those who had high positions of leadership within the cult were unable to "get out" for fear for their lives and those of their families.

The members of this cult did not become mass murderers and contract killers right away. In fact, many of them attended the meetings to participate in yoga and meditation exercises, an escape from the stressful schedules of their lives. They found Asahara Shoko's teachings beneficial to dealing with their difficulties in life.

Over the course of time, these members were required to give tons of money, a majority of their time and completely cut themselves off from the society around them. They were brainwashed and deceived into doing horrible crimes "for the good of their beliefs."

Satan is behind all of the evil actions that are around us, including this destructive cult. People stop seeking truth and want quick solutions to their problems. Sadly, they turn to the "spiritual" world of darkness rather than the light because they desire comfort rather than the truth of God. We need to be careful that we do not just follow our feelings in searching for the truth. Depending on what we desire, our hearts may lead our lives astray (Matthew 6:21).

The Bible shows us how a group of spiritual leaders in the Old Testament were deceived because they did not seek the counsel of the Lord. Their judgment was clouded by what they saw. Read the following scriptures about the Gibeonites. They were a people who lived in an area close to where the Israelites were. Because they were afraid of the Israelites, they resorted to a ruse to protect themselves. The Israelites failed to be alert to the possibility of being tricked.

However, when the people of Gibeon heard what Joshua had done in Jericho and Ai, they resorted to a ruse: They went as a delegation whose donkeys were loaded with worn-out sacks and old wineskins, cracked and mended. The men put worn and patched sandals on their feet and wore old clothes. All the bread of their food supply was dry and moldy. Then they went to Joshua in the camp at Gilgal and said to him and the men of Israel, "We have come from a distant country; make a treaty with us."

The men of Israel said to the Hivites, "But perhaps you live near us. How then can we make a treaty with you?" (Joshua 9:3-7)

The men of Israel examined the supplies and questioned the men of Gibeon but did not inquire of the Lord. They examined the evidence placed before them, and then they made their judgments based on what they saw and not on God's will. The scariest part is that these men were all spiritually mature men who had been leading Israel. The whole group made the wrong judgment together. It is one thing for one man or one woman to make a wrong assessment but another dilemma for a whole group to make an incorrect choice.

There is a story about a famous samurai who as a young boy went to a well-known teacher for his training. The teacher asked him to prepare a meal, and while he was cooking, the teacher surprised him by coming into the kitchen with a big stick and beating him up. Another time, he was asked to clean the outhouse, and his teacher arrived with a wooden paddle and beat him again.

The next time, the boy was ready. As he was sweeping, the teacher appeared from out of nowhere, but the boy took his broom and fought off his teacher.

These types of encounters continued for a few years until the boy's instincts became so sharp that a small anomaly in the air would alert him to an attack.

Women have strong instincts, and we rely on them quite a bit. God gave us special instincts because we are the supporters, the nurturers and the intuitive ones since, on the whole, we do not possess as much physical strength as men. This is not to say that we are weak and unable to protect ourselves, but a man can develop a "six-pack," or firm abdominal muscles, more easily than a woman. We are just not built that way.

On the other hand, because men are generally physically stronger, they rely on that aspect of their abilities more than women when it comes to survival. Thus, they think more logically and linearly rather than through intuition or insight. That is why we will often *feel* more in a given situation than men do.

There is a good and bad side to this wonderful gift that God has given us. Just as a man might rely on his *logic* in a situation, we women will rely on our *feelings*. Sometimes our perceptions are not accurate. We may read into a situation something negative that someone is thinking about us, and be hypersensitive and sometimes even touchy. At those times, we can be totally wrong. But if we are open about what we are feeling, the truth comes out in the end. It takes time as God's powerful hand works on our behalf.

There have been so many times in my life when I thought that someone didn't like me, but in actuality, they really admired me. Or times when I thought that someone liked me, but in reality, they were trying to be nice so that they could get something from me.

There are so many self-help books out there now that tell people not to assume anything. My simple advice is: Don't jump to conclusions. Assume the very best but then make sure to pray. God is the one who will reveal the truth to us in the end.

The Israelites needed God's guidance to see the true identity of these foreign visitors who claimed to have come from a great distance. But they assumed too quickly and drew inaccurate conclusions. They assembled around the Gibeonites to sample and to investigate their supplies, but they failed to inquire of the Lord (Joshua 9:14–16). Based on the outward appearance of the situation, they made a treaty with these foreigners. The sad fact is that the whole group ratified the treaty with an oath which bound them to keep the treaty under all circumstances. They were ensnared by the ruse of the Gibeonites. There was no escaping their mistake.

How many blunders have we made because of a lack of prayer and meditation on the Scriptures? How many times have we made impulsive decisions, believing that we had the best intentions? Sometimes, our difficult or crucial decisions involve our children and our spouses. Other times, if we are in church leadership, our decisions influence a great majority of members if not all of them. How much more, then, should we rely on God and on prayer to lead us in the right direction? Look at the result of the mistake that the leaders of the Israelites had on the rest of the group:

> So the Israelites set out and on the third day came to their cities: Gibeon, Kephirah, Beeroth and Kiriath Jearim. But the Israelites did not attack them, because the leaders of the assembly had sworn an oath to them by the LORD, the God of Israel.
>
> The whole assembly grumbled against the leaders, but all the leaders answered, "We have given them our oath by the LORD, the God of Israel, and we cannot touch them now. This is what we will do to them: We will let them live, so that wrath will not fall on us for breaking the oath we swore to them." (Joshua 9:17-20)

Unfortunately, the consequence of the leaders not inquiring of the Lord had resulted in the people being angry at them and distrusting their ability to make wise decisions. Leadership is a great responsibility before God and before the people who follow. When experience, knowledge and humanistic thinking take precedence over prayer and even fasting, God's guidance is nullified. Yes, it takes time to pray. Yes, it takes sacrifice to delve into the Scriptures for insight. And, yes, it is easier to make an impulsive decision rather than to put in the time to inquire of the Lord! Satan uses the excuse of a "lack of time" and "experience" to deceive God's people into taking shortcuts for important evaluations. This can be true for decisions we make for our family or our jobs as well.

Look at your life. Have you been willing to take the time and effort to discover the truth? Have you taken the time out to pray and to fast about crucial decisions in your life? Are you getting advice then bringing it before "God's altar" in prayer before taking conclusive action?

If so, continue to do so. Good for you. If you have forgotten these basics and have some important issues at hand to deal with, get on your knees like you once did. Remember, God is faithful and will show us the way. His desire is to always reveal the truth to us as long as we seek it.

> Seek the LORD while he may be found;
> call on him while he is near.
> (Isaiah 55:6)

7
SATAN ATTACKS SPIRITUAL PEOPLE

Satan has his sight set on those who are leading God's people. You may or may not have a leadership position in the church, but either way, we lead the people around us as a friend, a mother, a sister, a mother-in-law, a roommate, a daughter, and in many other roles. Satan wants to use each one of us to crush the faith of others—by our words, our actions and our example, or lack thereof.

If he can crush the person guiding people to Jesus, then he will be able to make many fall at once—a domino effect. Why do you think that Satan tried so hard to tempt Jesus on the cross? That one time, if Jesus had sinned, would have destroyed the chance for all of us to be saved! Satan uses sin as his weapon of mass destruction! He was determined to do whatever it took to manipulate and to entice Jesus.

Consequently, all the great prophets and leaders of the Bible have been targeted by Satan. Some of them fell for a time but rose again like King David after sinning with Bathsheba (2 Samuel 11). Some remained faithful even as they faced persecution, imprisonment, torture and death. They fought by hoping against all hope like Daniel in the lions' den (Daniel 6).

> In fact, everyone who wants to live a godly life in Christ Jesus will be persecuted, while evil men and imposters will go from bad to worse, deceiving and being deceived. (2 Timothy 3:12-13)

Let us look in the book of Zechariah. Here, the high priest is being accused by Satan. Satan is standing close by Joshua, the high priest, only to torment and to accuse him. There is not much known about this high priest, however, it is clear that he has sinned, because "his clothes were filthy" as he stood before the angel of God.

> Then he showed me Joshua the high priest standing before the angel of the LORD, and Satan standing at his right side to accuse him. The LORD said to Satan, "The LORD rebuke you, Satan! The LORD who has chosen Jerusalem, rebuke you! Is not this man a burning stick snatched from the fire?"
>
> Now Joshua was dressed in filthy clothes as he stood before the angel. The angel said to those who were standing before him, "Take off his filthy clothes."

> Then he said to Joshua, "See I have taken away your
> sin, and I will put rich garments on you!" (Zechariah 3:1-4)

The Lord was merciful to Joshua, the high priest. God rebuked Satan and saved Joshua like a "burning stick snatched from the fire." Though he had sinned, God was ready to help and to cleanse him of his sins.

Similarly, we are all "burning sticks snatched from the fire" through God's grace. Though we may be Christians, we are definitely not without sin. We can feel accused and unforgiven as we stand before the throne of God in prayer or at church. No matter how hard we try, we can "feel" like we have not been forgiven of our past sins. It is Satan who is standing there on our "right side" accusing us as he has accused all the spiritual men and women of the past.

Satan assaults women with accusations. We can be driving out to visit a friend and hear his voice, as Eve did, saying: *You are not good enough. You are a failure. You have nothing to offer.* His voice is loud. It rings in our minds and goes down to our hearts, a poison of the soul. It eats away at our faith and plunges us into a world of negativity and inaction, keeping us from having the impact that God wants us to have.

He also arms us with accusations which we bring against others through slander, gossip and critical attitudes, which often stem from hurt and disappointments within us. Satan will use our reckless words to accuse and to destroy. Let us not allow the Destroyer to take control of our conversations and, most of all, our heart.

All in all, it is imperative for us to pray for one another to grow and to change in areas that are less than perfect. Whether we are leaders or members in God's church, our prayers for one another will help each one of us to remain strong in our faith. It is only through working together and giving each other the benefit of the doubt that we will be able to overcome the challenges. Let us not allow Satan to taint our relationships. Remember that Jesus is the shepherd of all of our souls. He does not want us to imitate the accuser and accuse one another in hurtful ways.

❧

STUDY QUESTIONS

Satan: Does He Have Power Over Me?

1. Jesus calls Satan the prince of this world. He is also known as "the destroyer" (Revelation 9:11). As you think about Satan's power in this world and how he tried to destroy Job's life, consider the following questions in your life:

   a. How has Satan tried to destroy your life through sin and temptation as he tried to destroy Job's?

   b. Has your heart stayed righteous like Job's, or have you allowed bitterness and other sins to control you?

2. Satan has attacked spiritual people all throughout history and up to the present.

   a. Have you allowed Satan to accuse you through self-criticism and the criticism of others?

   b. Have you been praying for your friends and family to remain faithful?

3. Satan uses various weapons to make Christians fall. Although you try to resist, you will be greatly tempted to sin. Think about the ways that Satan tries to deceive you and answer the following questions.

   a. Which of Satan's weapons work against you most (see 1 John 2:15–17)?

      1) The cravings of sinful man

      2) The lust of the eyes

      3) The boasting of what you have and do

    b. How are you doing battling those challenging areas in your life?

4. Are you seeing what God sees, or do you believe the lies of Satan?

    a. In what ways does Satan convince you of his lies?

    b. What truths do you need to see with your heart?

5. There is a price to truth. It takes time and sacrifice to go to God. Many times, we want to take shortcuts and rely on our own intuition or feelings. All too many times, we rely on our past experiences and our earthly wisdom to help us see the truth when God is waiting for us to turn to him for guidance.

    a. Think about the areas of your life in which you rely on your own knowledge and experience. How much have you surrendered these parts of your life to God?

    b. Are there people like the Gibeonites in your life that have deceived you through their convincing arguments? What have you learned from your experience? What will you do differently in the future?

3

The Holy Spirit

How Does He Lead Me?

"But the Helper, the Holy Spirit, whom the Father will send in my name, he will teach you all things and bring to your remembrance all that I have said to you. Peace I leave with you; my peace I give to you. Not as the world gives do I give to you. Let not your hearts be troubled, neither let them be afraid."

John 14:26-27 (ESV)

1
The Workings of the Spirit

Did you know that the Hebrew word for the *Spirit* literally means "wind" *(ruwach)?* In the New Testament, the writers use the Greek word *pneuma* which means "breath or breeze." Does this make the Holy Spirit a *thing*? No, the Bible clearly portrays the Spirit as a being—the Spirit of God. But, for some reason, many people refer to the Holy Spirit as an "it." In sermons and classes, we learn a great deal about God and Jesus, but many times the Holy Spirit is rarely mentioned. In the Scriptures, there is clearly a trinity consisting of the Father, the Son and Holy Spirit. But where does the Spirit fit into the picture?

Most of us have seen the movie *Star Wars* in which the *Force* plays a major role. It is the invisible power present throughout the series. Often, we think of the Holy Spirit as a kind of *Force*. But just as God refers to his Son as "he," Jesus refers to the Spirit as "he." The Spirit is a being—a personality—in the same way God and Jesus are. He counsels (NIV) or comforts (KJV) (John 14:15–17). He teaches (John 14:25–26). He tells the truth or testifies about Jesus (John 15:26). He guides (John 16:13). He commands and creates (Genesis 1:1–2). He intercedes in prayer (Romans 8:26). He is *in you* (Romans 8:9)!

When we look closely, throughout the Scriptures, we see that the Holy Spirit is everywhere!

He was present at the creation of the world.

> In the beginning God created the heavens and the earth. The earth was formless and empty, and darkness covered the deep waters. And *the Spirit of God was hovering* over the surface of the waters. (Genesis 1:1-2, NLT, emphasis added)

He was present at the conception of Jesus Christ!

> This is how Jesus the Messiah was born. His mother, Mary, was engaged to be married to Joseph. But before the marriage took place, while she was still a virgin, *she became pregnant through the power of the Holy Spirit.* (Matthew 1:18, NLT, emphasis added)

He was present at the baptism of Jesus.

> After his baptism, as Jesus came up out of the water, the heavens were opened and *he saw the Spirit of God descending like a dove* and settling on him. (Matthew 3:16, NLT, emphasis added)

He was present at Christ's resurrection.

> The Good News is about his Son. In his earthly life he was born into King David's family line, and he was shown to be the Son of God when he *was raised from the dead by the power of the Holy Spirit.* (Romans 1:3-4, NLT, emphasis added)

He was present at the beginning of the Church on the Day of Pentecost.

> Peter replied, "Each of you must repent of your sins and turn to God, and be baptized in the name of Jesus Christ for the forgiveness of your sins. *Then you will receive the gift of the Holy Spirit.* This promise is to you, and to your children, and even to the Gentile—all who have been called by the Lord our God." Then Peter continued preaching for a long time, strongly urging all his listeners, "Save yourselves from this crooked generation!"
>
> Those who believed what Peter said were baptized and added to the church that day—about 3,000 in all. (Acts 2:38-41, NLT, emphasis added)

And he is still with us today!

Dear sisters, haven't you always wanted someone to really understand you? Someone who really knew you and still accepted you as you are? Someone to whom you could tell all your secrets, and who would, in turn, tell you all their secrets? Someone who gives freely to you and never holds back from you? Someone you feel completely safe with?

> But it was to us that God revealed these things by his Spirit. *For his Spirit searches out everything and shows us God's deep secrets.* No one can know a person's thoughts except that person's own spirit, and no one can know God's thoughts except God's own Spirit. *And we*

have received God's Spirit (not the world's spirit), so we
can know the wonderful things God has freely given us.
(1 Corinthians 2:10-12, NLT, emphasis added)

Hanging out with God's Spirit is like hanging out with your best friend. You whisper secrets to each other. He understands your thoughts. He knows how you feel. He tells you the deep secrets of God. He gives willingly and completely. He is always with you, knowing all your fears, all your insecurities, all your joys, all your hopes and dreams. He is familiar with all your ways.

> You know when I sit down or stand up.
>   You know my thoughts even when I'm far away.
> You see me when I travel
>   and when I rest at home.
>   You know everything I do.
> You know what I am going to say
>   even before I say it, LORD.
> You go before me and follow me.
>   You place your hand of blessing on my head.
> Such knowledge is too wonderful for me,
>   too great for me to understand!
> *I can never escape from your Spirit!*
>   I can never get away from your presence!
> (Psalm 139:2-7, NLT, emphasis added)

His Spirit surrounds us, enveloping us with his unconditional love. There is nowhere you can go to hide from the Holy Spirit. Even before you speak a word, he knows what you are going to say…yes, he even knows when you mess up! He knows you completely and follows you far and wide. He lives inside of you—your body is his temple (1 Corinthians 6:19). You are never alone. He will follow you into death and lead you to your eternal home, because he is eternal.

So it is with you. When you heard the true teaching—the Good News about your salvation—you believed in Christ. And in Christ, God put his special mark of ownership on you by giving you the Holy Spirit that he had promised. That Holy Spirit is the guarantee that we will receive what God promised for his people until God gives full freedom to those who are his—to bring praise to God's glory. (Ephesians 1:13-14, NCV)

I have a very cute little dog named Kumo. He is an adorable, white and fluffy Maltese. From the moment I wake up in the morning, that little creature watches my every movement. Even though he may be in a deep sleep, if I get up to go to a different room, he will jump up to follow me. When I am in a bad mood and ignore him, he still wags his tail and shows me unconditional love. When I am alone at home and a bit scared, I cuddle up next to him, and he doesn't mind a bit, but loves every moment he can be near me.

Of course, there may be those of you out there who are not dog lovers, but the point is that it is a nice feeling to have a loyal, loving and faithful friend beside you all the time. The Holy Spirit is more than a devoted pet animal. He is more than a reliable friend. He is more than a loving husband. He is more than a boyfriend. He will even give you special gifts, which we will talk about later in this chapter.

Dear sisters, open up your heart and your mind to allow the winds of the Spirit to blow through your heart, your mind and your soul—to lead you, instruct you, love you, direct you and teach you. Think about him today and every day as you walk together with him on your journey. Let his power be revealed in you and through you.

2
LIVING TO PLEASE THE SPIRIT

The front door crashes open.

A second later it slams shut.

It's your husband. Another bad day. You go over to give him a kiss, but he ignores you. He gives you no love. You don't want to deal with him anymore. Your love fizzles out like a dying match.

"Where's my jersey?" shouts your teenage son. "You always wash it on the days that I need it!"

You look frantically for the jersey and finally find it.

There are no thank you's, only a grunt. Then, you hear his footsteps running out to the garage. The car starts and whizzes away with a loud skid. You cringe at the sound. He doesn't come home until the middle of the night. You peek in to see your sleeping son, but the room reeks of alcohol. You wonder where your cute little boy disappeared to. There used to be so much joy in watching him sleep, but not tonight.

The mailbox is filled with envelopes. No, there's no card in there—only bills. You check your bank account. Not enough to pay all of them. Suddenly, the anxiety wells up inside. There's no peace.

The bathroom scale is sitting on the floor. You haven't weighed yourself in a week. You close your eyes as you step on. You hear the needle spring back and forth a bit. You wait a few seconds before you open your eyes.

"What? How can that be? There's no way I could have gained that much weight in a week! I only cheated once during Thanksgiving."

That's it. You're done. Nothing is working.

No more patience.

When life hits, it hits hard. No more nice feelings. No more warm fuzzies. We get fed up. We lose it. We want to give up. It's too hard. Yet, as we go through our ups and downs, did you know that the Holy Spirit sympathizes with us? That's right: Just like you and me, he feels joy, disappointment, excitement and sadness. However, his responses are not based on the circumstance but on our reaction and motives. We can make the Spirit grieve by our actions (Ephesians 4:30). We can please him (Galatians 6:8). We can hurt him by quenching his power (1 Thessalonians 5:19). Yet, he stays with us and lives in us all the time.

> Guard the good deposit that was entrusted to you—guard it with the help of *the Holy Spirit who lives in us.* (2 Timothy 1:14, emphasis added)

Dear sisters, most of us desperately desire to be loving, joyful, peaceful and patient during times of testing—but all too often, the grinding reality of our daily lives can turn these attitudes into little more than a far-off dream. This is why we need to turn to the Holy Spirit.

> So I tell you: Live by following the Spirit. Then you will not do what your sinful selves want. Our sinful selves want what is against the Spirit, and the Spirit wants what is against our sinful selves. The two are against each other, so you cannot do just what you please. (Galatians 5:16-17, NCV)

But how can we live to please the Spirit when we can think that daily life makes it almost impossible to make the right decisions?

First of all, we need to see that God's Spirit makes his home in us. He will stay put with us, through the good and bad times. He does not leave when our lives become more demanding. He does not come and go on the basis of our perfection or lack of it. He is always there working on our behalf and helping us to grow as Christians. For this reason, we must realize that he is the one who produces fruit in our lives—not we ourselves.

> But the Holy Spirit produces this kind of fruit in our lives: love, joy, peace, patience, kindness, goodness, faithfulness, gentleness, and self-control. There is no law against these things! (Galatians 5:22-23, NLT)

In the scripture above, there are nine outcomes of living to please the Spirit. None of these are from our own power. It clearly says that they are produced by the Holy Spirit. How humbling is that? We cannot take any credit for being loving, joyful, peaceful, patient, kind, good, faithful, gentle or self-controlled. All of these qualities come from the Spirit inside of us! When we are filled with the Spirit and live according to the Spirit, these traits will be reflected in our lives.

It is interesting how the word *fruit* is a singular word in the scripture. That means it signifies more than just one characteristic, describing an overall result of how we live. Sometimes we might think, *If only I could be more loving,* or *If only I had more patience...* Actually, through the Holy Spirit, we have that possibility...and more. As we live to please the Spirit, all those qualities fill us at once—and in increasing measure! Yes, when you have one, you have them all!

Wait!

Don't get all insecure and feel that if you don't have all of the fruit of the Spirit that you are a failure. That is not how it works. God gives us all the Spirit, and when we strive to live for Christ, he will bear fruit through our lives. At first, the Spirit's fruit may only seem like a feeble presence. Later on, as we grow, the fruit grows more and more evident. When we learn to be controlled by the Spirit rather than by our sinful nature, which previously had control over us, the Spirit brings life to us with the fruit of his righteousness. We set the Spirit free to work in our lives as we make godly choices:

> But you are not controlled by your sinful nature. You are controlled by the Spirit if you have the Spirit of God living in you. (And remember that those who do not have the Spirit of Christ living in them do not belong to him at all.) And Christ lives within you, so even though your body will die because of sin, the Spirit gives you life because you have been made right with God. (Romans 8:9-10, NLT)

The Spirit will become more active as we learn to acknowledge his presence and please him. Yes, we are still going to have our struggles. And yes, we will sin again and again, but this does not mean that God's Spirit will leave us. This is where God's grace takes over. We need his power to help us.

When I used to watch the cartoon show *The Flintstones,* I would laugh at the way Fred drove his car with his bare feet. In a similar way, when we were in the darkness, we lived life on our own humanistic power, like virtual Fred Flintstones, "driving" our lives barefoot. We tried to live as "good" people, but without the power of the Holy Spirit, we were like a woman trying to move or stop a heavy car with her bare feet. We ended up failing, hurting ourselves and others in the process. Of course, we tried hard. Of course, we had no intention of hurting others. But later on, we realized how we had fallen short and it made us humble before the cross.

Thank goodness, in real life we have cars with fancy engines and a braking system (whose inner workings are a mystery to me!). God knew that it would continue to be a struggle for us to live righteously, so he gave us his Spirit. Now we are "driving" our lives with an ultra powerful engine and power brakes—no more bare feet—just a push on the pedal and away we go! We are the fancy car with an amazing engine—even if we can't quite explain how it all works. It is important to note that we still need to push the pedal (i.e., make the right choices), but then the Spirit grants us ability beyond our own strength to live out those righteous decisions.

We need the Holy Spirit—the same power that raised Jesus from the dead! It takes that much power to keep us on the right path:

> And *if the Spirit of him who raised Jesus from the dead* is living in you, he who raised Christ from the dead will also give life to your mortal bodies through his Spirit, who lives in you. (Romans 8:11, emphasis added)

This means that we have an incredible amount of power available to us that we may not be aware of. If we could fathom just a small amount of the tremendous power that the Spirit could work inside of us, we would probably be astounded.

Some scientists estimate that we, as human beings, only use ten percent of our brain at any given time. There are others who say that the actual percentage is even less—closer to six percent. Yet, researchers seem to agree that although we physiologically have the potential use of one-hundred percent of our brain, we never tap into all of it at once. For instance, there are parts of the brain used for repair work when someone has a stroke. We don't use those parts all the time, and perhaps, never. Other sections are used during times of trauma or emergency when adrenaline shoots through our bodies. During those times, our mind, body and organs function at a higher level due to the brain working harder. There are still other areas of the brain whose role or function scientists do not completely understand. These workings of the brain remain a mystery.

One factor is clear about the brain: We can help it to function better by eating well, being happy, learning new information, meeting interesting people, etc. The brain gets energized and works more powerfully when we use it. It has remarkable powers that scientists are still researching and trying to fully grasp.

In the same way, the potential of the Holy Spirit's power in a Christian's life far exceeds that which we can imagine. Most, if not all, of us have barely tapped his ability to transform our lives. Although his work may seem mysterious, we can help the Spirit to work at his best as we feed ourselves spiritual food through the Word, learn about him, keep a positive attitude and become close to people who can help us to grow spiritually. He will then produce more fruit in us as we live to please him. When there are difficulties and times of extreme stress, the Spirit will kick in—leading us, teaching us, encouraging us, strengthening us—in ways that we cannot quite comprehend:

> And the Holy Spirit helps us in our weakness. For example, we don't know what God wants us to pray for. But the Holy Spirit prays for us with groanings that cannot be expressed in words. And the Father who knows all hearts knows what the Spirit is saying, for the Spirit pleads for us believers in harmony with God's own will. And we know that God causes everything to work together for the good of those who love God and are called according to his purpose for them. (Romans 8:26-28, NLT)

Isn't the Spirit astonishing? He wants to work in us and produce fruit in us. He gives us all the power that we need to live for our Lord. Without him, we are truly powerless and weak. We have been blessed with a wonderful gift.

3

LEARNING TO BE LED BY THE SPIRIT

Decisions. Decisions. Decisions.

Dear sisters, are you in the middle of a big decision in your life? Or will you have to make a crucial choice in the near future? Somehow, life gets more complicated and less clear as we grow older. What seemed to clearly be "God's will" at one point in time may seem to be a huge mistake a year or two later. What may have been a key factor in all of our decisions a few years ago may not be an issue any longer. What we may have relied on or trusted in for years can no longer be our guide, because those factors are simply no longer valid. Most of the time there are no simple answers. And with age and time, everything gets clouded by our past experiences, whether good or bad.

With life full of so many choices, how do you make the right decisions? What if there seems to be no right choice? When the option seems beneficial financially, is Satan or God behind it? How can you tell whether you are being tempted or led? No matter what alternatives are presented in our lives, God gives us his Holy Spirit to be our counselor, our guide and our teacher. When we allow ourselves to be led by the Counselor, we will be able to discern what is best.

How do we learn to follow the Spirit? Through surrender. Surrendering to Jesus is a part of our walk with Christ. Sisters, we can become spiritual packrats. We don't forget our bad experiences very easily—we pack them away in our hearts and vow never to forget.

Others of us have accumulated many physical "valuables" along the way as Christians—we like where we are and don't want to let go of anything more than we have to. Suddenly, when God asks us to give up some of our valuables for him, we realize how firmly we have been clinging on.

The cross we started out carrying as young Christians has been put aside out of so-called "practicality" or "level-headedness." Gradually, the cross becomes a mere symbol rather than the true sacrifice of Christ—a sacrifice we are called to embrace. We are not eager to do "spiritual" acts, viewing them as nothing but busyness without depth. And all this does not make us a Spirit-led woman. We are, in fact, led by a schedule rather than by the Holy Spirit. No wonder some of us don't feel fulfilled in doing his work. We are running on empty.

Surrendering our will to Jesus allows him to direct our lives through the Spirit. This means that we do not put any conditions on God. Even as Jesus called his disciples, he urged them to follow him with all of their heart. There is no such thing as a "half Christian." The commitment to Christ is one-hundred percent:

> Then he called the crowd to him along with his disciples and said: "If anyone would come after me, he must deny himself and take up his cross and follow me. For whoever wants to save his life will lose it, but whoever loses his life for me and for the gospel will save it." (Mark 8:34-35)

Jesus calls us to a discipleship that denies self and that takes up our cross daily in order to follow him. This is more than adhering to a program of spiritual activity—it is an attitude and condition of our hearts. What is your cross today? Has it become too heavy? Have you dropped it along the way and decided to go into "survival" mode? Do your responsibilities take precedence over your commitment to the heart of the cross? If we want God to guide our path, then we must be willing to follow in his steps of surrender, not where our feelings go.

Just like a ship held in shallow waters by an anchor, we can become immovable spiritually, even though we want to fulfill God's plan for our lives. According to Jesus, we must get rid of any anchors that we have placed in our lives. Many of these anchors take root without us realizing it. Some of the anchors come from our desire to have a "stable" and "comfortable" life. As women, we like to have our little nest all in place—our schedule, our home, our finances and our family. Of course, there is nothing wrong with that desire, but these things can become obstacles that keep us from giving our very best to Jesus. They can cause us to compromise in our giving and our willingness to sacrifice for others.

Another anchor is bitterness and negativity; both lead us to dark places as we get caught up in how others have treated us. These attitudes unchecked produce failed relationships. Jesus knows our hurts and our disappointments. Yet, he desires us to remain steadfast in following him. Jesus continued to be vulnerable, knowing that he would be hurt. He does not ask us to do anything that he has not already done himself. He calls us to a life that imitates his heart and his example (1 John 2:3–6). In this way, we can be strengthened and encouraged to lift up our cross, joyfully forgiving and letting go of the bitterness.

Often, we are not aware of the anchors stalling out our faith. In fact, until God reveals them through certain incidents or people, we can be completely oblivious to the true condition of our hearts. Most of us want to be transformed through God's Holy Spirit and yet often feel frustrated by our flesh.

Time and time again, our weaknesses creep into our lives and make us stumble. We do not want to sin but end up finding ourselves going from one mess to another. This is why we need to pinpoint our anchors so that we can pray about them specifically. Less obvious anchors can be fears, insecurities, resentment, frustration and feelings of being trapped.

Yet, God gives us many great promises so that we can confidently haul up our anchors and trust in him. Even the apostle Paul struggled with his sins and weaknesses. He did not want to sin but would end up falling repeatedly (Romans7:15–25). It was only through the power of Jesus Christ and the Holy Spirit that he was able to overcome.

As we go through life battling to make important and often complicated decisions, we will learn to face our anxieties and weaknesses, and see that God has great plans for us (Jeremiah 29:11–14). Always remember: the Holy Spirit is trying to direct us in the right path. Prayers for guidance will be answered as we seek God with all our hearts.

> Know that the LORD has set apart the godly for himself;
> the LORD will hear when I call to him. (Psalm 4:3)

> Those who know your name will trust in you,
>   for you, LORD, have never forsaken those who seek
>   you.
> (Psalm 9:10)

As we grow in our understanding of how the Holy Spirit works in our lives, we begin to feel his comforting guidance. When the burdens become too heavy, the Holy Spirit takes over to help us lift up those anchors out of our heart and surrender our fears to him.

Let the wind of the Spirit blow into your life and direct you like never before. This wind will blow where it pleases—accept that you are not in control of your life. Though you may hear its sound, you might not be able to discern where it comes from or where it will take you.

No matter what, remember that you are born of the Spirit—a special gift from the Lord. He wants you to benefit from that power as he intended. Let us release the anchors and allow the Spirit's power to blow us in the direction of his will and not our own.

4
WHAT HAPPENS IF I DON'T FOLLOW THE SPIRIT?

The Holy Spirit directs us, but he does not force us to do what is right. In fact, sometimes we know what we *should do* and still go against it, but the Spirit allows us to make our mistakes. He is a perfect guide, yet one who never coerces us to respond.

At the same time, there are decisions that have nothing to do with right and wrong. We may face a choice based on our preference or desire. For instance, we can get accepted into two great schools, or we may receive two different job offers, both incredible opportunities, but we can only take one of them. After struggling through these choices, however, we can be wrought with regret a few months or years down the road. Thoughts like: *What if I had accepted the other job instead?* or *I should have chosen that other school; then I would have been happier,* end up haunting us.

Then, there are other kinds of decisions in which we feel like we had no choice because we were at the mercy of someone else. Those are the times we feel like we were forced to go in a certain direction in life, and so we blame others for the unhappiness we experience.

For instance, you may be married to a spouse who is not a Christian. He might have received a promotion which took your family to a city where you knew no one. Or you may have borrowed money from a relative, and now they expect you to do a favor for them that would compromise your faith. Is it Satan setting up a situation where he can plant seeds of bitterness in your hearts? What role does the Spirit play in these kinds of situations?

Dear sisters, many of us have been burned, hurt, betrayed and deceived into circumstances that we did not want to be in. Unfortunately, life is unfair in such ways, whether at the workplace, at church or in school. But as adults we don't have to be weak and pressured into doing things or forced into being a certain way. We have a choice and always will have one. We just need the courage and the strength to move forward with what God's Spirit tells us to do. Look at the prayer of David's psalm:

> Show me the right path, O LORD;
> point out the road for me to follow.
> Lead me by your truth and teach me,
> for you are the God who saves me.
> All day long I put my hope in you.
> Remember, O LORD, your compassion and unfailing love,
> which you have shown from long ages past.
> Do not remember the rebellious sins of my youth.
> Remember me in the light of your unfailing love,
> for you are merciful, O LORD.
>
> The LORD is good and does what is right;
> he shows the proper path to those who go astray.
> He leads the humble in doing right,
> teaching them his way.
> The LORD leads with unfailing love and faithfulness
> all who keep his covenant and obey his demands.
> (Psalm 25:5-10, NLT)

I have made my share of mistakes in my life. Before God's Spirit entered into my life, I made stupid decisions—decisions that have left scars to this day. In fact, I was rebellious in my youth. As a teenager, I was involved in many sins. Because I did not grow up with any set of morals or a faith of any kind, I did as I pleased. My only boundary was my parents' anger. As long as they didn't know or didn't get too angry at me, I made my own decisions. My actions were a result of my selfishness and my pride.

After becoming a Christian, however, I didn't change all my sinful habits nor did I cease to make mistakes in my life. Sometimes, the sinful side of me takes control, whether it is my selfishness, pride or my lack of faith—at those times, I make decisions based on my feelings, my insecurities or my hunches rather than through the guidance of the Holy Spirit. Furthermore, I sometimes pray for God to bless decisions that I have already made, without really thinking about whether the Spirit is leading me or not.

Becoming a Christian doesn't make any of us into perfect beings. Sometimes, our weaknesses will take over, not allowing the Spirit to work fully in our lives. So we will make mistakes and make the wrong decisions even though we might have the right intentions. Having the right intentions does not make us sinless. We will even allow the influence of others to make us stumble and go in the wrong direction because we were too weak to stand up and do what was right. When we look at the disciples after Jesus leaves them, we see them make mistakes and even sin.

Sisters, haven't we all had our moments when we have not wanted to obey what Jesus commanded?

Instead of apologizing, we have continued to argue.

Instead of forgiving, we have held a grudge because we weren't convinced that the other person was really going to change.

Instead of being patient, we have pushed our agenda through because no one else seemed to care.

Instead of loving someone, we have pulled away because we are not in the mood.

God gave us his Spirit so that we could see what was true. If we sit still, close our eyes and pray for the truth to be revealed, we will see it clearly.

The Spirit says, "Yes, it was not that person's fault alone."

The Spirit whispers, "Please don't stay angry."

The Spirit admonishes us, "Please forgive even if the person doesn't ever change."

The Spirit encourages us, "Don't pull away. Keep giving. I am with you. You can do it."

The world does not want to accept the Spirit. It rejects his teachings, his leading and his admonishments. They do not know him or see him. But God's Spirit is with you, inside you and knows you deeply. He knows your motivations. He sees your fears. He acknowledges the unfair treatment. He recognizes all your hurts. He accepts you as you are—a child of God. Although he will allow you to make your mistakes, he will try to prompt you through different ways so that you will not continue in the wrong path.

In the New Testament, the Spirit guided, warned and directed the apostles. All the paths were not easy ones. Just because you undergo suffering does not mean that Satan is in control. Sometimes, the Spirit leads us on difficult paths:

> "But when he, the *Spirit* of truth, comes, he will guide you into all truth. He will not speak on his own; he will speak only what he hears, and he will tell you what is yet to come." (John 16:13, emphasis added)

> "The *Spirit* told me to have no hesitation about going with them. These six brothers also went with me, and we entered the man's house." (Acts 11:12, emphasis added)

> When they came to the border of Mysia, they tried to enter Bithynia, but the *Spirit* of Jesus would not allow them to. (Acts 16:7, emphasis added)

> "And now, compelled by the *Spirit*, I am going to Jerusalem, not knowing what will happen to me there. I only know that in every city the Holy Spirit warns me that prison and hardships are facing me." (Acts 20:22-23, emphasis added)

God spoke to Pilate's wife in a dream. She warned her husband not to have anything to do with the innocent man. But Pilate was caught in the middle. The crowds surrounding him shouted out, "Crucify! Crucify!" (John 19:4–6). Pilate found no basis to condemn such a man. Yet, it was up to him to arrive at the final verdict. He had the authority to save Jesus' life. He, however, felt the pressure of the crowd as they shouted for Jesus to be crucified. Understandably, Pilate felt trapped in this situation. He desperately tried to convince the crowd to spare Jesus and to condemn the notorious criminal, Barabbas, instead.

Sometimes we know the truth. Yet, the words of the pushy and opinionated people win out. It can be very difficult to carry out what is right. We can fall into the trap of giving in because we do not have the strength to fight back. In addition, we can be driven by fear and conflict-avoidance rather than by righteousness. The pressure of a group can truly be deadly. Convincing arguments and strong voices can force us to make the wrong decision for ourselves and for those we love.

Pilate was trapped between what he knew to be right and his reputation as governor. Pilate washed his hands before the crowd to make amends for his actions. This did not, however, release him of his responsibility before God.

> When Pilate saw that he was getting nowhere, but that instead an uproar was starting, he took water and washed his hands in front of the crowd. "I am innocent of this man's blood," he said. "It is your responsibility!"
>
> All the people answered, "Let his blood be on us and on our children!"
>
> Then he released Barabbas to them. But he had Jesus flogged, and handed him over to be crucified. (Matthew 27:24-26)

In the Old Testament, there is another example of a bad choice made by a man of faith; his name was Samson. He wanted to marry a certain Philistine woman. This went against the laws of Moses, yet he commanded his parents to get her for him (Judges 14:1–3). God, however, had plans for this as it had actually been a part of God's plan to conquer the Philistines:

> At that time, the Philistines were in control of Israel, and the LORD wanted to stir up trouble for them. That's why he made Samson desire that woman. (Judges 14:4, CEV)

Believe it or not, God knows us so well and has planned into his design all our mistakes! Since he recognizes our faults, being our Creator of course, he even allows our wrong decisions to work into his plans! That is how his Holy Spirit can work in us as well. Wow, this means that even our bad choices can be used by God! Isn't it amazing how God's love interweaves our mistakes to be a part of his greater plan? God had a better plan when Pilate washed his hands and allowed Jesus to go to the cross. God had a better plan when he allowed Samson to choose a woman from the uncircumcised Philistines to be his wife.

In the New Testament, the apostle Peter also made a terrible choice the night before Jesus was crucified. Jesus even warned Peter that before the rooster crowed, he would deny him three times (Matthew 26:34, Mark 14:30, Luke 22:34). When Peter was told about his imminent denial, he insisted that he was ready to die for Jesus (Matthew 26:35, Mark 14:31, Luke 22:33). Sadly, that same night, Peter faced his weakness—his cowardice with a servant girl the first time, then another girl the second time! He denies his Lord and gives in to his fears—not just once, but three times! Unlike Judas, however, Peter took responsibility for his mistake, and it changed his life forever. He was the first of the apostles to run to Jesus' tomb when news of his resurrection arrived.

Peter could have blamed the servant girl who recognized him as one of his disciples (Matthew 26:69). He could have made excuses about the second girl (that she was six-feet tall and scary looking) (Matthew 26:71). He could have even criticized the other disciples for not defending him when he cut off the high priest's servant's ear, trying to protect Jesus (John 18:10). He could have also rationalized about how he had been very busy and extremely tired, so he was just not at his best (Matthew 26:40). Instead, he owned his sin and repented. So when Jesus rose from the dead, Peter felt the freedom to jump into the water and swim to Jesus. He knew forgiveness and had no hesitation at the sight of his risen Savior (John 21:7).

In contrast, Judas responded to his mistakes by running away. He received thirty pieces of silver, which he tried to return to the temple because he felt remorse over his actions (Matthew 27:3). Yet, when the chief priests would not accept it back, he decided to kill himself (Matthew 27:4–5). His wrongful deeds would have been forgiven by Jesus. But instead of taking responsibility, Judas would not face his mistakes. He felt alone and in distress. In his mind, he had nowhere to turn with his actions being beyond forgiveness—thus, his suicide.

Despite all our weaknesses and frailties, God has a plan through his Holy Spirit to use our mistakes and moments of disobedience to him. As we live out our lives trying to be our best for the Lord, the Spirit will sometimes allow us to go to unpleasant places in order to see our flaws and, hopefully, change them. Not only that, but God can use our wrong choices for even greater purposes. The Spirit rejoices when we are willing to fully accept responsibility for our choices. When we do, our mistakes can truly be used to glorify God.

5

THE GIFTS OF THE SPIRIT

As I write these words, Christmas is just around the corner. I love gifts. I love giving them and receiving them. Even though I intellectually understand that Christmas is not all about gifts, one of my "love languages" is gifts. That means I feel loved when someone takes the time out to think of a special gift for me. It does not have to be expensive. In fact, it can be a card or a single flower. But it makes me feel all warm inside, knowing that the person thought about me.

The Holy Spirit knows that we, women, like gifts. He is a gift-bearing being—full of surprises! In fact, the Holy Spirit is himself a gift. He was given to us from God and manifests in us through different ways. But that doesn't mean that we each receive a different Spirit.

> There are different kinds of spiritual gifts, but the same Spirit is the source of them all. There are different kinds of service, but we serve the same Lord. God works in different ways, but it is the same God who does the work in all of us.
>
> A spiritual gift is given to each of us so we can help each other. (1 Corinthians 12:4-7, NLT)

God has given us the *same* Spirit, but he works in different ways through each of us. These gifts are given to us so that we can share them with each other and not so that we can use them for ourselves. There may be some of you reading this and thinking that you don't have a spiritual gift and that God forgot to give you one when he gave you the Spirit. This is not so! Every one of us has been given a spiritual gift:

> Each person is given something to do that shows who God is: Everyone gets in on it, everyone benefits. All kinds of things are handed out by the Spirit, and to all kinds of people! The variety is wonderful.
> (1 Corinthians 12:4-7, The Message)

This is a translation from the Message Bible. It makes it so clear that everyone "gets in on it, everyone benefits." That means that none of you women out there were left without a spiritual gift. But it is the Spirit who decides when, where and who gets what gift. This giving of gifts never makes one person more important than another. In fact, Paul warns us not to think of ourselves more highly than we ought as he teaches about the different gifts (Romans 12:3). No gift ever makes us better than someone else nor does the lack of a gift make us less than someone else. These gifts are given, not to build ourselves up, but to build up the Church (Ephesians 4:12).

You may want a certain gift from God and have a desire to serve in a certain way, but that may not be the Spirit's will. This does not mean that God loves you less than the person who has that gift. And it also does not mean that the person is smarter, more talented or more blessed. It is all according to God's grace. The fact that we have any gift at all is a blessing from the Lord.

> We have different gifts, according to the grace given us. If a man's gift is prophesying, let him use it in proportion to his faith. If it is serving, let him serve; if it is teaching, let him teach; if it is encouraging, let him encourage; if it is contributing to the needs of others, let him give generously; if it is leadership, let him govern diligently; if it is showing mercy, let him do it cheerfully. (Romans 12:6-8)

Imagine if everyone had the same gift because it was the "most popular" thing to have. What would happen to the church? It wouldn't be fun if everyone was fighting to get up at the pulpit and preach. It would be horrible if everyone wanted to lead with no one to follow. What would we do without the generous people in the church? What would happen if the brothers and sisters in the body who love to serve were no longer there? What would happen to our faith if the encouraging people all disappeared?

These spiritual gifts are different from our talents and level of education. It does not take a Harvard degree to be generous. It does not require an Olympic medal to be serving. If this were the case, our pride would take over, not allowing the Spirit to manifest himself fully in our lives. Sisters, let us not have a worldly perspective on the gifts given by the Holy Spirit. They have nothing to do with our IQ, physical abilities or worth. In this way, we can rejoice and be thankful for those with the ability to preach, teach, lead and to govern, understanding that it is completely through the grace of God that anyone is allowed to do so.

So we do not need to struggle with insecurity about how much God loves us or how useful we are in the church. Whatever gift you have is a special gift given to you, according to God's grace. We can pray to God so that we can use our gifts to help others. We can ask for guidance from the Spirit to know how we can best help the church by exercising our gifts. We can even ask other Christians for input as to how we might help the people around us.

Of course, we could talk about each gift and its uses. Others have written insightful books about how to know what gifts we have and how we can use them for the church. But that is not the purpose of this chapter.

The point is that the Holy Spirit is a gift-giver. Every day is Christmas for a disciple of Jesus because the Spirit never stops giving his gifts. This was all at the cost of our Lord Jesus who was nailed on the cross for our sins. He gave us the greatest present—the forgiveness of sins. Not only that, but he also gave us a deposit guaranteeing our salvation through the Spirit. When we were born again of the water and the Spirit, we became temples of God's Holy Spirit so that God lives in us everywhere we go.

> Jesus answered, "Truly, truly, I say to you, unless one is born
> of water and the Spirit, he cannot enter the kingdom of

God. That which is born of the flesh is flesh, and that which is born of the Spirit is spirit. Do not marvel that I said to you, 'You must be born again.' The wind blows where it wishes, and you hear its sound, but you do not know where it comes from or where it goes. So it is with everyone who is born of the Spirit." (John 3:3-6, ESV)

The Spirit is blowing inside of you. His breeze cascades within the essence of your being. He enters inside the depth of your heart, prompting you, guiding you, teaching you and strengthening you. He dances around your soul, rejoicing with your faith, singing with your heart and celebrating your salvation. Do you hear him blowing inside your soul?

His gifts are laid before you, ready to be used, ready to build up the church and ready to help shape the faith of others. Do you see them working in your life?

His fruit is poured out as a bounty at harvest time—the kindness, the love, the patience, the gentleness, the joy—all the qualities that exhibit his existence inside of you. Do you feel his prompting to do what is righteous and pure?

You don't know where he will blow and where he will take your life. You are born of the Spirit, and the Spirit loves you and caresses you with his power. So, dear sisters, be Spirit-led women—women who listen to his counsel, women who use his gifts for the church, and women who bear much fruit through the Spirit.

✍

STUDY QUESTIONS

The Holy Spirit: How Does He Lead Me?

1. The Holy Spirit is inside of you. He is always with you. He knows all your thoughts and your feelings—both good and

bad. After reading this chapter, in what ways have you changed the way you view the Holy Spirit in your life? How can you be more conscious of his presence with you?

2. The Spirit bears fruit in our lives as we learn to please him. How have you been trying to live to please the Spirit?

3. Through the help of the Spirit, we can make the best decisions in life. What decisions have you made recently in which you relied on God's Spirit to guide you?

   a. How are you doing in surrendering to God's will in your life?

   b. Has your commitment to Jesus been one-hundred percent, or have you found compromises in your life that keep you from holding on to the right decisions?

   c. What "anchors" do you find in your heart that keep you from surrendering completely to God?

4. We all make mistakes in our lives. The Holy Spirit moves in our hearts so that we can learn from them. Many times, however, we find it challenging to take responsibility for our shortcomings. What are some mistakes or failures that have helped you to grow and to mature as a Christian? Are you open about sharing those weaknesses?

5. The Holy Spirit is a gift-bearing being. He gives us these gifts so that we can help to build up the church as well as help those around us. What do you think are your gifts?

   a. Look at the gifts of the Spirit in your life. How have you been using them for God and his church?

   b. If you are not sure what your gifts are, ask a friend or someone close to you to help you see what they are. Then pray to God for guidance through the Spirit about how you can use them.

4

Demons

ARE THESE EVIL SPIRITS
STILL ACTIVE TODAY?

A good friend of mine who was a missionary in India told me an extremely scary story about the power of demons. You may have your doubts, but consider what happened. One evening, during a Bible study group, a young man came to her home. He had been attending church for quite some time and had begun studying the Bible. Even though he had been interested in becoming a Christian, it was difficult for him to consider truly converting from Hinduism. He had been a devout Hindu his whole life, going to temples every day and chanting the mantras, engaging in the idolatry involved in his worship. His family members were very upset with him going to church, and so they put a curse on him.

That evening this young man participated in the Bible study group, and suddenly, became possessed. He was a quiet person by nature, and physically quite slight. He started growling in a loud weird voice claiming to be a demon. He mentioned the name of the demon (my friend does not remember the name), and he spoke in the first person, as if he was the young man. Then, the young man became violent, picking up large pieces of furniture and throwing them around. He was doing things he ordinarily could never have done. The Christian brothers jumped on him and began rebuking the demon. This went on for about ten minutes; then the demon finally left. The young man went home, and they never saw him again.

Later that night strange things started happening in my friend's house. The doorbell would ring, and when they would go to the door, no one would be there. It happened several times.

Then they would be standing in a certain room, and the lights would go on and off, when no one was present. This continued to happen for several days.

My friend told me that people there do all kinds of crazy things under the influence of demons. They cut themselves, carry out child sacrifices, and put curses on people. There was even another young man, an acquaintance of hers, who had slit his own throat and lived to tell the tale.

As Christians, whether we live in the United States or in another country where Christianity is not the primary religion, we must be aware of the influence of demonic forces. If we had special eyes to spiritually see what was really happening around us, we undoubtedly would be shocked. Our struggles with our faith are not simply doubts and uncertainty about God's word; there is a very real spiritual battle going on around us for control of our lives. Paul describes the battle in no uncertain terms:

> Our struggle is not against flesh and blood, but against the rulers, against the authorities, against the powers of this dark world and against the spiritual forces of evil in the heavenly realms. (Ephesians 6:12)

1

ARE DEMONS REAL?

Where did demons come from? If they are still around, how active are they today? What do demons do to us? How do they affect our lives?

Many times Christians use the term "demons" and "Satan" interchangeably. Demons, however, seem to have their own identity, apart from Satan. The word "demon" comes from the Greek word *daimon,* which is derived from the verb *daiesthai* meaning "to divide, distribute." In the Hebrew Bible, there seem to be two classes of demons, *se'irim* and *shedim.*[1] The *se'irim* ("hairy beings") were faunlike spirits to which some Israelites offered sacrifices in open fields.

There are several different views of what these evil spirits are. According to some cultures, they are souls of departed evil people appearing as ghosts or spirits. Josephus, a first-century historian and apologist of priestly and royal descent, spoke of demons as "spirits of the wicked which enter into men that are alive and kill them."[2]

Others believe that they are the spirits of the offspring of angels and women.

In the Bible, demons act like "evil" angels, misleading and deceiving their victims. (We'll take a closer look at the link between demons and angels in this chapter.) Yet, unlike angels, some of these spirits seem to possess people, rendering them self-destructive. In the Gospel accounts, their possessed victims often lived in cemeteries, leading several scholars to believe that some demons are souls of the dead who feel "comfortable" around the dead and even want to kill their hosts out of jealousy for their being alive.

No matter what their origin, demons are definitely for real.

2
WHAT DO THEY DO?

According to the Scriptures, demons seem to be beings that follow Satan and do his evil bidding. The New Testament describes them as fallen angels who took the side of Satan when he rebelled against God (Revelation 12:9) or as angels who have sinned (2 Peter 2:4, Jude 1:6). In fact, they were instrumental in helping Satan rebel against God and Christ. They were thrown to the earth alongside Satan after the war in heaven.

> And there was war in heaven, Michael and his angels
> waging war with the dragon. The dragon and his angels
> waged war, and they were not strong enough, and there
> was no longer a place found for them in heaven. And the
> dragon was thrown down, the serpent of old who is called
> the devil and Satan, who deceives the whole world; he
> was thrown down to the earth, and his angels were
> thrown down with him. (Revelation 12:7-9, NASV)

In this scripture, Satan's servants are referred to as "his angels." These "angels" were thrown down on this earth by the archangel Michael. Consequently, they inhabit the earth and are functioning as instruments of evil around us. As we mentioned before, Satan was also an angel in heaven—probably the most influential of them all. Many say that he might have been an archangel like his counterpart, Michael. His control, however, was limited since he was merely an angel and not God. God is omnipotent and omniscient—having all supremacy and wisdom. He sees all and knows all.

On the other hand, Satan and his demons have to roam the earth looking for people to manipulate and deceive (Job 1:7). Unlike God, they do not know everything. The Scriptures even indicate that some demons are being held in Hades in anticipation of the final judgment (Jude 1:6). So take heart, dear sisters, they are limited in their powers.

3
DEMONIC ACTIVITY

As Christians, we might have dabbled in the occult by visiting a psychic "for fun" or by looking at our astrology chart to see if it is accurate. In all likelihood, for most of us, nothing ever came of those predictions except a few laughs or coincidences. However, some start believing in the power of the occult and can even begin to *rely* on it.

The dark world is real and has an ability to draw in certain types of people. Those people are often discontent with their church or religion. They might have had some disappointments in their lives, making them doubt their faith. For this reason, they seek their answers from some "mystical" powers rather than from God. Those people feel like there is more to the spiritual world than what they see and hear at church—and, most likely, there is. But when we allow ourselves to be "open" to other beliefs, we begin to cross the threshold into dangerous territory.

One example of the "power" of psychic abilities or fortune-telling takes place in the book of Acts:

> Once when we were going to the place of prayer, we were met by a slave girl who had a spirit by which she predicted the future. She earned a great deal of money for her owners by fortune-telling. This girl followed Paul and the rest of us, shouting, "These men are servants of the Most High God, who are telling you the way to be saved." She kept this up for many days. Finally Paul became so troubled that he turned around and said to the spirit, "In the name of Jesus Christ I command you to come out of her!" At that moment the spirit left her. (Acts 16:16-18)

Paul encountered this fortune-teller, whose spirit immediately recognized the Holy Spirit inside the disciples of Jesus! She told the truth about Paul. But it troubled Paul, so he rebuked the spirit and cast it out of the girl. Though prophets in the Bible also foretold the future, those predictions were given to them from God, not from some unknown spirit. The spirit that Paul casts out of the fortune-teller was obviously not of God; it was most likely of demonic origin as it could be cast out of the girl.

In the same way, Jesus encountered and cast out demons

throughout his ministry. It seems that a vortex of evil entered into the world to wage war against the good in Jesus and the plan of redemption that God would work through him. Of the seventy-two references to demons in the New Testament, sixty-two occur in the Gospels. (Which, by the way, likely means we have less demonic activity today.) Casting out demons was as much a part of Jesus' ministry as healing the sick, feeding the poor and preaching the good news.

He saw evil spirits in people. He sometimes addressed them directly as he interacted with the victims. For this reason, demons were afraid of him. Since Jesus understood how they worked, he taught the disciples about them and warned them about how they possessed people:

> "When an evil spirit comes out of a man, it goes through arid places seeking rest and does not find it. Then it says, 'I will return to the house I left.' When it arrives, it finds the house unoccupied, swept clean and put in order. Then it goes and takes with it seven other spirits more wicked than itself, and they go in and live there. And the final condition of the man is worse than the first. This is how it will be with this wicked generation." (Matthew 12:43-45)

One fact is clear from this scripture: Demons seem to make their home in people and in objects. One person can even have several demons possessing him or her, as seen in Mary Magdalene (Luke 8:2) and the demon-possessed man at the tombs (Luke 8:26–31).

As Christians, we do not talk about demon-possession very often. When people behave in a wicked manner, we rationalize it as some psychotic problem. Yesterday I heard on the news that a woman had chopped off both her little girl's arms and allowed her to bleed to death. What kind of mother could commit such an atrocious act? While all mental illnesses or physical ailments may not be the work of demons, we cannot totally rule out the possibility of demonic activity in certain people's lives.

Jesus saw past the person and could identify Satan and his demons inside of individuals. When he saw them, he addressed them directly, never addressing the person being possessed, but rather the possessor:

> Jesus turned to Peter and said, "Get away from me, Satan! You are a dangerous trap to me. You are seeing things merely from a human point of view, not from God's." (Matthew 16:23, NLT)

> Jesus responded, "Haven't I handpicked you, the Twelve? Still, one of you is a devil." He was referring to Judas, son Simon Iscariot. This man—one from the Twelve—was even then getting ready to betray him. (John 6:70, The Message)

> Then Satan entered Judas, called Iscariot, one of the Twelve. (Luke 22:3)

> When Jesus saw that a crowd was running to the scene, he rebuked the evil spirit. "You deaf and mute spirit," he said, "I command you, come out of him and never enter him again." (Mark 9:25)

Demons even possessed children. If Jesus saw the devil and demons in people, should we not also be aware of their working in people's lives? The comedian Flip Wilson (as Geraldine) is famous for the statement, "The devil made me do it." Though the Scriptures teach that our own sinful desires make us sin (James 1:13–15), a portal to evil spirits is open to people who allow sin or sinful hearts to control them. So, there may have been some truth in what "Geraldine" said. It is only through Christ's power that we can overcome the work of such malevolent spirits. Let us never be naïve to the work of demons in this world.

4
DON'T BE LED ASTRAY

Did you know that demons are also responsible for false teachings? This is a powerful way that demons lead multitudes astray.

> The Spirit clearly says that in later times some will abandon the faith and follow deceiving spirits and things taught by demons. Such teachings come through hypocritical liars whose consciences have been seared as with a hot iron.
> (1 Timothy 4:1-2)

The teachings of demons are in conflict with the teachings of God. Yet, sadly, these demonic philosophies will often seem logical to many who listen. Many will abandon the faith to follow hypocritical teaching. Therefore, we must examine not just the words but also the life of a teacher or an individual who influences us spiritually (Hebrews 13:7). Of course, no one is perfect, but if someone is visibly living against the teachings of God—talking the "spiritual" talk but walking contrary to God's law, the Bible warns us to be aware.

The only way to differentiate between "God" and "demonic" activities is through the fruits of a life. What may seem like the light, can actually be part of the darkness:

> For such men are false apostles, deceitful workmen, masquerading as apostles of Christ. And no wonder, for Satan himself masquerades as an angel of light. It is not surprising, then, if his servants masquerade as servants of righteousness. Their end will be what their actions deserve.
> (2 Corinthians 11:13-15)

Demons—sometimes working through people—are out to mislead and demolish our faith. Like an ocean wave eroding the side of a cliff over many years, Satan and his demons work to slowly erode our godly way of life until there is almost nothing remaining. They will target our weaknesses through false teachings and half-truths that make us believe that we are "fine" when, in actuality, we are drifting from God and his word.

Let us not be unaware. Demonic forces are able to scheme, to reason and to make their own decisions with the purpose of confusing and deceiving the most intelligent among us. They deceive us into sinning. Then, we get caught up in the cycle of bad habits. Christ came into this world to destroy our evil way of life and to destroy sin.

> Dear children, do not let anyone lead you the wrong way. Christ is righteous. So to be like Christ a person must do what is right. The devil has been sinning since the beginning, so anyone who continues to sin belongs to the devil. The Son of God came for this purpose: to destroy the devil's work. (1 John 3:7-8, NCV)

As we mentioned earlier, Jesus taught that demons are looking for a "home" that is unoccupied. In fact, they are constantly looking for victims. When they find someone, they make their home within him or her. In the New Testament, the man who had a legion of demons inside him was drawn away from people to solitary places (Luke 8:27–29). Once a demon or a group of them gets a hold on someone, they do not want to let go. They especially do not want their victims around others who can help them. The forces of evil want to isolate their victims in order to maintain complete control over them.

Sisters, this is important! The spiritual world of evil wants to draw its victims away from spiritual people. Demons always recognized

Jesus. They recognized Paul and the other disciples. They will recognize you, who have the Holy Spirit inside! They feared the Christ who had power over them and could subdue them. They spoke to Jesus and begged them to have mercy on them. The legion of demons even beseeched Jesus not to torture them (Mark 5:7). Obviously, fellowship with other women (and men!) in Christ is essential to protecting our hearts from the influence of spiritual evil.

As women, we can be led astray by our emotions and by our desires, though not all emotions and desires are evil or demonic in nature. Often it is our longing to be loved or our desire for security which can cloud our judgment and blind us to the truth. When we allow those feelings to take control, we open the door for the demonic forces to direct us down the wrong path. Even those of us who may have been Christians for many years are not immune to wandering from God and hardening our hearts. In fact, some who have been in the faith a long time can tend to possess hearts turned numb to the goodness of God. The temptations are always there and will present themselves when we are the weakest.

> With the Lord's authority I say this: Live no longer as the Gentiles do, for they are hopelessly confused. Their minds are full of darkness; they wander far from the life God gives because they have closed their minds and hardened their hearts against him. They have no sense of shame. They live for lustful pleasure and eagerly practice every kind of impurity. (Ephesians 4:17-19, NLT)

When demons take control of people, they want to bring harm to that person—not good. The demon-possessed boy was thrown into the fire and into the water often (Matthew 17:15). He was physically tortured by seizures as well. Demons made men cut themselves with stones and other sharp objects, giving them little or no sleep (Mark 5:5).

Demons are insatiable in their desire to occupy a living being. Even when Jesus cast out the legion of demons from the man, they begged Jesus to let them go inside a herd of pigs. Like parasites, they wanted to be inside of a living creature—even a herd of pigs. They were desperate to possess and feed off of their victims—maybe craving their life energy—then to destroy them. We see this as the pigs run off the cliff to their deaths. It would seem that they are actively roaming and constantly looking for their next victim. Given how terrible possession is, victims who are healed are very grateful (Luke 8:38).

As seen in the above Gospel accounts, actions that are self-destructive are many times derived from demonic influences. Many women in today's world who want to lose several pounds resort to anorexia and bulimia to look "beautiful"—anything to attract the opposite sex or to give them self-confidence. In reality, all these obsessions pull us away from God. They can become a type of addiction. The thoughts and teachings about looking thin are all lies from Satan and his demons. It is a fixation on our weight, our bodies and our looks—not a passion for God.

Again, we cannot clearly say that eating disorders mean that a person is possessed by a demon. But we can see that Satan is working through lies to confuse and to destroy someone's life.

Merrill Unger in *What Demons Can Do to Saints*[3] discusses this question of Christians and demonic influence on the human mind. Unger claims that Christians can have their mental state negatively influenced by demons and sometimes this can be to a significant extent. While the devil cannot force any of us to do anything that we do not want to do, as we have mentioned earlier, Unger reasons that mental problems can be caused both by medical conditions and by demonic activity.

Many of these "addictions" or disorders stem from depression and inner turmoil. While all of these may not originate directly from demonic activity, evil spirits can use these weaknesses in people to worsen their condition. There may actually be a legitimate medical condition, but, as Christians, we must see how demonic activity can influence matters to degenerate. This may not be actual demon-possession as we see in the New Testament, but rather demonic forces at work to hurt the individual through self-destructive methods.

Then, there is the guilt, the hopelessness and depression that follow all these sinful patterns. It is a cycle that can trap our minds and our hearts. God tells us that our bodies are a temple of the Holy Spirit, so we must honor God with our bodies and not abuse them to satisfy our longings to look attractive (1 Corinthians 6:19–20). We cannot allow the demonic powers to harm our thinking, then our bodies.

If these are areas that you fall into from time to time, be open. Don't be afraid to get help. Don't let the demonic forces take control and isolate you—making you live in secrecy rather than in the light. God is light. In him, there is no darkness at all (1 John 1:5). God asks us to live in the light and not allow the darkness to overtake us.

Satan and his demons are influential, but they cannot prevail over God. It is up to us to decide to fight. Just as Satan worked through Peter to tempt Jesus (Matthew 16:23), Satan and his demons may use people in our lives to try to convince us to do the wrong things. We must learn to recognize these malevolent forces and engage in battle against them.

5
RESIST AND PRAY

From what we have read of Satan and his demonic legions, we should expect that they will attack our hearts, tempting us with negative and sinful thoughts. Mix those temptations with a bad day and wild emotions, and we can easily spiral down in our faith. God wants us to win the fight with these forces of evil, though it may be extremely difficult. Hence, the Bible gives us strategies:

> Submit yourselves, then, to God. *Resist the devil,* and he will flee from you. Come near to God and he will come near to you. Wash your hands, you sinners, and purify your hearts, you double-minded. (James 4:7-8, emphasis added)

This scripture tells us to submit to God and to resist the devil. We must refuse to give in to the devil. When Satan and his demons begin to take control of our feelings, we have a choice: to submit to God or to submit to the dark forces of this world. If we let emotional reactions reign, we often end up saying and acting in ways that are contrary to what we would desire.

Then, the cycle begins. Our accused consciences beat us up over and over for our mistakes. There seems to be no escape during those times. That's why we need to remember the exhortation of James: Submit to God and resist the devil! No matter how hard our day has been, no matter how hard the temptations may become, even when we are weak—if we submit to God, he can help us to overcome. He has given us the authority and power we need.

Some of us may be asking, "But how do I fight when I get too weak to fight?" The answer I've found is prayer. Ironically, often one of the last things we do is to pray. We allow our hectic lifestyle to keep us from going to God for strength. Sometimes, all it takes is for us to get down on our knees and beg God for guidance and help. If we are still feeling weak, we can call a friend and ask her to pray with us. There is nothing more powerful than our prayers, whether in solitude or in union with others.

The James 4 scripture promises us that if we come near to God, he will come near to us. When we draw away from God in anger and frustration, we fall into the devil's trap.

Satan and his demons do not want us women to know that we have already won the battle against the dark forces of this world. We, in fact, have authority over them. Jesus has already won the victory for us (John 16:33), and he gave us the victory alongside him when we believed and made him Lord of our lives.

> You, dear children, are from God and have overcome them, because the one who is in you is greater than the one who is in the world. (1 John 4:4)

> For everyone born of God overcomes the world. This is the victory that has overcome the world, even our faith. Who is it that overcomes the world? Only he who believes that Jesus is the Son of God. (1 John 5:4–5)

Unfortunately, instead of recognizing the authority we have in Christ, we tend to focus on simply appeasing our consciences. We busy ourselves with chores, responsibilities and with other commitments in our lives. Later on, when we have time to think, the guilt-laden accusations of our hearts keep us awake at night, giving us little or no sleep. Before we know it, we find ourselves controlled by the cycle of our frazzled life and our guilty consciences, and we become too weak to stand firm and weather the challenges.

Yes, the small ways we try to numb our guilt can give an opportunity for the dark forces to slowly pull us away and cause us to harden our hearts. We need to believe that God loves us and wants the best for us. He will not give up fighting for our souls. God will use his people to intervene and to help us at the right time. At those times, we should be eager for the help of Christians and God himself in order to stand strong.

6

IDOLATRY AND DEMONS

Finally, did you know that the Bible links idolatry with being influenced by demons? Take note of this surprising passage:

> So, my dear friends, flee from the worship of idols. You are reasonable people. Decide for yourselves if what I am saying is true. When we bless the cup at the Lord's Table, aren't we sharing in the blood of Christ? And when we break the bread, aren't we sharing in the body of Christ? And though we are many, we all eat from one loaf of bread, showing that we are one body. Think about the people of Israel. Weren't they united by eating the sacrifices at the altar? What am I trying to say? Am I saying that food offered to idols has some significance, or that idols are real gods? No, not at all. *I am saying that these sacrifices are offered to demons, not to God. And I don't want you to participate with demons. You cannot drink from the cup of the Lord and from the cup of demons, too. You cannot eat at the Lord's Table and at the table of demons, too.* What? Do we dare to rouse the Lord's jealousy? Do you think we are stronger than he is?
> (1 Corinthians 10:19-22, NLT, emphasis added)

While we were in Tokyo as missionaries, we became friends with a woman whom we called Grandma Hashizume. She became a Christian during the initial years of our stay in Tokyo. Before becoming a Christian, she was a devout Buddhist and Shinto and prayed to her idol daily. She believed that her husband was inside the idol, waiting each day for her to speak to him.

As we studied the Bible, however, she understood that idolatry was a sin. She was an eighty-year-old woman who had lived her whole life believing in her pagan traditions, but through the Scriptures God showed her that the Lord of heaven and earth had no form or image (Deuteronomy 4:15–19).

Grandma Hashizume took down her little *butsudan* or altar which housed her idol and burned the small image. In doing so, she was able to see that the idol was just a wooden object and gained a deeper conviction of its evil. For many years, almost her entire life, it had captured her heart and devotion, making her believe that it could guide and save her. She replaced her idol with her Bible, making her little wooden altar into a small cabinet for her church books and journals. She was so proud of her new modest bookshelf with pretty wooden doors! She learned to hate idolatry because of the grip that it had on her life.

> Cursed is the man who carves an image or casts an idol—a thing detestable to the Lord, the work of the craftsman's hand—and sets it up in secret. Then all the people shall say, "Amen." (Deuteronomy 27:15)

Just as idolatry was detestable to God, it also became detestable to Grandma Hashizume, and she denounced every area of her idol worship. She remained faithful to Jesus until the very end of her life. In fact, the day before she died, she asked my husband and me to come and have lunch with her. Of course, she had no idea that she was going to die the next day. She brought her daughter, who was also a Christian, to the restaurant to help her get there and back home.

During that mealtime, Grandma Hashizume wanted to make sure that she was right with God. She had been having doubts about her faith. If she could believe a lie for eighty years, what was to prevent her from putting her faith into another lie before her death? She wanted to make sure that the Bible was really the truth.

My husband, Frank, was patient with Grandma Hashizume as he shared some scriptures and reassured her that her choices had not been a mistake. He recounted all the ways that God had worked in her life since she had become a Christian. As he reminded her of each and every event, she began to cry, realizing how foolish she had been to doubt. She went home so encouraged and excited about her faith. That night, she prayed that she was ready to be with God whenever he wanted to take her, because she had no more doubts.

The following morning, Grandma Hashizume woke up with a headache, fainted and fell down the stairs. She was rushed to the hospital in an ambulance. Her daughter called me, and I went to the hospital to meet them. Her whole family was in tears as they stood around her bed. By then, Grandma Hashizume was in a coma. As soon as I arrived, I grabbed her hand and spoke to her, hoping that she could understand me. Somewhere I heard that people in comas can sometimes hear.

"Grandma Hashizume, if you can hear me, wiggle your toe," I said to her.

Almost immediately, she began to wiggle her toe. The whole family was shocked to see that she could hear. Yet, that was the only part of her body that she seemed to be able to move. Then, I reassured her that she was going to be all right. I repeated the words that my husband had told her the day before. I also encouraged her by telling her that her faith was stronger than ever.

Grandma Hashizume went to be with her Lord that very night. She held on to her faith to the very end, despite her fears. She overcame the hold that idolatry had on her, making Jesus her Lord. She won the final victory and met her Lord. I cannot wait to see her again in heaven.

Sadly, in many countries of the world, the deception of idolatry pulls people far away from the truth—more than we could possibly imagine. It was a powerful evil that had a tight grip on Grandma Hashizume. And it has a firm grasp on the hearts of many people outside of Christianity—whether Hindu, Shinto, Buddhist or others. The fact that these powerful beliefs in idolatry have such an intense influence over billions of people in the world, makes God angry.

When I lived in Japan, we had to constantly redefine God to the Christians because an unseen and imperceptible God was such a foreign concept. All the gods that the Japanese had grown up with were tangible and visible to them. Because of this, they had a constant need to find something tangible in order to have faith in the unseen.

Being brought face to face with the beliefs in the Japanese culture, I have gained a deeper conviction about the evil of idolatry. It creates distance from God and makes our Maker into a small and weak object. In Japan, people believe that gods can be made and carried with them from place to place. The value of the idol is based on how it was crafted—whether with stone, gold or silver. The object is not the Creator but the creation of the created. An idol can break apart and even rot, while our God is exactly the opposite—an eternal and everlasting being:

> Who compares with God? Is anything like him?
> Is an idol at all like God?
> It is made of bronze with a thin layer of gold, and
>   decorated with silver.
> Or special wood may be chosen because it doesn't rot—
> then skilled hands
> take care to make an idol that won't fall on its face.
> Don't you know?
> Haven't you heard?
> Isn't it clear that God created the world?
> God is the one who rules the whole earth, and we that
>   live here are merely insects.
> He spread out the heavens like a curtain or an
>   open tent.

God brings down rulers and turns them into nothing.
(Isaiah 40:18-23, CEV)

God cannot be made into or likened to a small object. What an insult to such a great and strong Creator! It would be like someone borrowing our car and thanking our car rather than us! People worship these idols believing that they house the spirits of their dead. They sacrifice to them—not like in the past with the blood of people or animals—but with food, gifts and money. Though the Bible refers to such idols as gods, they are not God. There is a difference between these so-called "gods" and the one true God of the heavens and the earth. Those who worship these false gods give them—and demons—power in their lives through their belief in them.

They made him jealous with their foreign gods
and angered him with their detestable idols.

They sacrificed to demons, which are not God—
gods they had not known,
gods that recently appeared,
gods your fathers did not fear.
(Deuteronomy 32:16-17)

Friends, this is where some of us may need to beware of how demons are working to weaken our faith today. Perhaps, you live with a form of Christianity where idols are a part of the worship—incense and statues of "gods" to whom you pray. Such practices can cloud and compromise our ability to see the truth. No matter what appearance or shape a statue or image may have, Jesus Christ should have no form except that spoken of in the Bible.

Idolatry can take many other forms, as well. Maybe you do not bow down to an idol or worship a statue...but are there cravings in your heart that take precedence over your relationship with God?

The problem in American society today may not be the worship of carved stone or molded plaster, but rather an idolatry of another form. Many "Christians" have fallen away from God in their hearts. They might not have consciously decided to leave God, yet their love for God and their priorities in their relationship with him have taken a backseat. God is no longer the driver or the inspiration in their lives. The demons of idolatry are at work manipulating their lives.

> Then the word of the LORD came to me: "Son of man, these men have set up idols in their hearts and put wicked stumbling blocks before their faces. Should I let them inquire of me at all? Therefore speak to them and tell them, 'This is what the Sovereign LORD says: When any Israelite sets up idols in his heart and puts a wicked stumbling block before his face and then goes to a prophet, I the LORD will answer him myself in keeping with his great idolatry. I will do this to recapture the hearts of the people of Israel, who have all deserted me for their idols.'
>
> "Therefore say to the house of Israel, 'This is what the Sovereign LORD says: Repent! Turn from your idols and renounce all your detestable practices!'" (Ezekiel 14:2-6)

The Bible teaches clearly in the book of Ezekiel about men who had set up idols in their hearts. These idols had become stumbling blocks in their lives. They believed that these idols were actually God, which deceived them into thinking they were faithful. The Jews had drifted from true Judaism into a form of godliness that compromised their faith. God was angry with the Israelites. He desired to have their full heart, not just a part of it. In the same way, we can lose our "first love" for the Lord. We might love God but not with the same passion and fervor that we did when we first became Christians.

God is immeasurable and magnificent, supreme and powerful; therefore, he can never be reduced to a mere piece of wood or metal.

He should never be second to anything in this world. He is unmatched and limitless—far beyond human understanding. Consequently, let us not allow the demons of this world to erode our faith by diminishing our God into false representations or materialistic possessions or dreams and ambitions that aren't centered on him. We must be vigilantly careful not to replace our worship of the one true God with other "important" priorities in life.

Demons are real...but they are not in control. In a spiritual world, surrounded by spiritual forces of evil, we must keep our eyes on Jesus. We are not alone, and we are not powerless. Christ has won the victory, and through him, we have the ability and the authority to resist evil.

~

STUDY QUESTIONS

Demons: Are These Evil Spirits Still Active Today?

1. In reading about demons, what did you learn? How was your understanding of them different from what the Scriptures teach?

2. Demons can lead us astray. We need to learn to discern in all circumstances whether it is truly God who is leading us or whether there is demonic activity. Have you been resisting the demons that try to deceive you? Are there areas in your life that you have kept hidden from others? Decide today that you will bring those areas of struggle into the light so that the demonic forces cannot have power over your life.

3. Idolatry can be present in our lives in different forms. It is not just statues and images of God that can pull us away from our relationship with the Lord. It is whatever we place above our relationship with our Maker. What are some of the idols in your life that can keep you from having God as the priority?

a. What motivates you to keep Jesus Lord of your life? Think about these things and write them down.

b. Do you still have the same passion and gratefulness for the grace of God as you did when you became a Christian?

c. If you feel that you need more help in your understanding of God's grace, take time out to ask another Christian who is strong in their faith to help you find answers in the Scriptures.

4. Pray today for God to subdue the demonic forces around you so that you may overcome and can claim the victory that you already have in Christ.

Angels

ARE THEY TRULY AROUND ME?

Are not all angels ministering spirits sent to serve those
who will inherit salvation?

Hebrews 1:14

1

ANGELS, CHERUBIM, SERAPHS AND ARCHANGELS

Wouldn't it be nice if we could see these ministering spirits and watch them working in our lives? Wouldn't it be exciting to actually be aware when we are helped by angels? We would feel so much safer and more confident in life, just knowing that these spiritual beings are acting on our behalf.

Even as I watch TV, there are so many testimonials in which people describe "unexplained" phenomena—their daughter was saved from a fire—their little boy was "carried" away from a car accident—their lives were saved because they "heard" a voice calling them out from a dangerous situation which could have killed them.

Skeptics say that these occurrences are just coincidences, a moment of delusion in a crisis, or plain made-up stories for which there is another logical explanation.

Was Joseph, Jesus' father, delusional when he saw an angel in his dream warning him to leave Bethlehem? Was it just a coincidence that Hagar, Sarah's slave girl, heard an angel speak, leading her to water when she and Ishmael were dying of thirst in the desert? Is there a logical explanation for the angels who announced Jesus' birth to the shepherds out in the fields? Is the account of an angel speaking to Mary about her virgin birth a made-up story? Was Peter hallucinating when he was released from prison by an angel, or was it just a nice jailer who wanted to let him out?

If we deny these stories, we deny the veracity of the Bible. In fact, the Bible does not mention these stories in passing as if they were insignificant facts, but rather most of the accounts are told as major events that changed the course of a person's life. We can look at these "angel" narratives as true reports from God's people, written by the hand of God, or we can be like most of the world and believe them to be nice bedtime stories for children.

More than half of the books in the Bible mention some kind of angelic being. References to angels appear throughout the entire Old and New Testaments, sometimes describing in elaborate detail their actions, appearance or words. Jesus encountered angels during his time on earth—during his forty day fast (Mark 1:13) and after his all-night prayer before going to the cross (Luke 22:43). So who are these heavenly creatures, and what is their role in our lives?

Most of the time, we only talk about angels, but, according to the Bible, there are many other kinds of heavenly beings, including cherubim, seraphim and archangels! *Cherub* is the singular form of *cherubim* derived from the Hebrew word *kerub*.[1] They are cited numerous times in the book of Ezekiel. *Seraphim* or *seraphs*, meaning "burning ones,"[2] are technically only mentioned in the book of Isaiah but are also present in Revelation. In the Scriptures, only one archangel or "chief angel" is mentioned by name, Michael, but there seem to be other leading angels. Daniel mentions Michael as "one of the chief princes" (Daniel 10:13), indicating that there are other angelic higher-ups. Another angel, Gabriel, is mentioned in the book of Daniel and Luke but no apparent rank is indicated.

These celestial entities appear to have various shapes and forms, ranging from multifaced creatures (Ezekiel 1 and 10) with animal bodies to human-like beings (Hebrews 13:2). Each of them seems to have a specific role in fulfilling God's plan and purposes.

Cherubim are found guarding the holy articles and sacred places of the Lord. They are first mentioned in Genesis as guardians of the Garden of Eden. Two cherubim were placed at the east entrance of the Garden of Eden with a flaming sword flashing back and forth to guard the tree of life. In Ezekiel's vision, they support the throne of God (Ezekiel 10:1) and are standing in the temple of God (Ezekiel 10:3). Their images appear on the ark of God (Exodus 25:21, 2 Chronicles 5:8). These special "angels" may have also served as guards of the holy articles of the Jews.

Seraphim or seraphs are winged creatures given the role of praising God's holiness. They are referred to in the book of Isaiah (Isaiah 6:2–4) and Revelation (Revelation 4:8). Isaiah has a personal encounter with a seraph, in which the being seemed to have the power to convey forgiveness of sins. In Isaiah 6, one of them flies to Isaiah and touches his lips with a piece of burning coal to take the guilt of his sins away. Their appearance is not described in detail since their faces are covered by two of their six wings. Their voices ring out as they praise the Lord's holiness.

Though God often spoke directly to his people, at times God also used these heavenly beings to communicate with individuals, whether in dreams or in real life. After the book of Genesis, increasing encounters with angels are recorded. These appearances have no direct correlation to a person's faith, talent or position in society. Most of the time, these angels do God's bidding as messengers under God's command to herald an important event in history.

Angels seem to play an important role in relation to Jesus Christ as well. In the New Testament, the book of Hebrews begins with references to angels as compared to our Lord Jesus. God created angels to be inferior to Jesus. He commands the angels to worship the Lord in the first chapter. In the second chapter, the writer describes how God made Jesus a little lower than the angels when he sent him on the earth. Later, however, Jesus was crowned with glory and honor because he suffered death, making him superior to angels by name and majesty. Hebrews ends with brief remarks about angels in chapters 12 and 13.

The New Testament ends with the book of Revelation depicting angels as principle agents ministering to the churches. Some of them exist around the throne of God while others are aiding God in pronouncement of judgment on the people of the earth—both good and evil sentences. There are many references to them throughout this last book, showing their significant role in God's heavenly kingdom. Their presence is certainly noteworthy in God's spiritual world.

2

ANGELS EXIST TODAY

Angelic beings are not only present during biblical times but exist today and play an important role in every Christian's life. We may or may not be aware of their presence, but according to the book of Hebrews, they are sent as ministering spirits to those who are to inherit salvation (Hebrews 1:14). That means that every Christian is being ministered to by angels! What we may consider as a coincidence may be the work of angels, visible and invisible. Strangers that appear to help us out at just the right moment may actually be an angelic spirit that God has sent to assist us in our time of need.

Most often, we consider unexplainable incidences as happenstance. There may have been a person who helped you out in a precarious situation, and you have never seen him or her again. There may have been a stranger who arrived at a certain place when you were having difficulties. Maybe, you had a broken down car at night with no cell phone, but somehow your car just seemed to start working again after a quick prayer. You might have been a small child when someone you had never seen before guided you out of a burning building. Was it really chance or was God sending someone to watch over you at that point in time?

My husband and I lived in San Francisco for eleven months from August of 1987 to July of 1988. It was an exciting time in our lives. The church there helped us heal in our faith after we had faced several discouraging situations in the European mission field the prior year. It was an important time period because unknown to us at the time, God was going to call us again into the mission field before even a year had passed.

The ministry staff members in San Francisco were older and more experienced than Frank and I were. I was only twenty-three years old at the time. Because of our youth and inexperience, the whole staff knew that we needed God's help to make up for what was lacking. We needed to rely on God through prayer, fasting and confession of sins. Whatever experience we lacked would be taken care of by God.

In view of this realization, I personally made a commitment to have a prayer time with the Lord every Monday afternoon from 1:00 to 5:00. Each Monday, I would go to a special place in the San Francisco area where I would not be disturbed during those four hours. It became an adventure for me to find new places where I would be inspired by God's creation.

On one particular afternoon, I had found a beautiful hillside area in a national park across the Golden Gate Bridge in Sausalito, a cute town on the outskirts of the city. While gazing at the panorama of the bay, I passed three wonderful hours reading the Psalms, praying and singing hymns by myself. The weather was perfect, and the sun shone brightly.

I was feeling quite encouraged and happy when, suddenly, a lone hiker came walking up the hill toward me. At first, I was not worried. Yet, as he approached, I became very nervous. There was no one else in the vicinity to help me if something bad were to happen.

After a few minutes, panic began to set in as the hiker came closer and closer. I began to pray about what to do. My car was a good ten-minute walk away. There were no cell phones at the time and not a soul around to hear me cry out if I got into trouble. Furthermore, I had many books with me: two Bibles, a concordance, a hymnal and a notebook of prayers. I pondered how could I run fast with all these books and make it back to my car.

Then, it was too late. Before I knew it, the man was looking down at me as I sat there on the grassy hillside. He did not smile or greet me in a friendly manner as I had wished he would. In fact, he had a very serious look on his face and began to speak.

"Look at that boulder down at the bottom of the hill near you," he quietly said.

I shot a glance down the slope, wondering what he was going to say about it. He continued, "There has been a man hiding behind that rock with a knife. I think that he is after you. You need to get up slowly and follow me quickly down this hill. As you walk around this path, past the boulder, look back and you will see the man with a knife."

I was extremely shaken by his words. I did not hesitate, gathering up my belongings as fast as possible. Moving quickly, I followed the hiker down the hill on the winding dirt path. There was a bend where I could see behind the boulder as I passed by. Sure enough, there was a man crouched down behind the stone outcropping. Apparently, he was not aware of my departure from the hillside. He seemed to be waiting and holding something in his hand. Fear gripped me as I stared at the stranger and caught a glimpse of his knife flashing in the sunlight!

When I looked ahead of me to follow the man, the hiker had disappeared. He was nowhere to be found, neither in back of me nor around me. That was it. Gripped with fear, I began to run as fast as I could. Thoughts of my body floating in the San Francisco Bay under the Golden Gate Bridge seized me as I wondered whether I had been tricked. *Were those men actually working together to ambush me down at the bottom of the hill? Where is the man who warned me? How could I have lost him so quickly?*

No matter where I looked, the man was gone—out of sight. Poof! Disappeared into thin air, it seemed, because there was no other path. When I finally got to the bottom of the hill, I rushed to my car. My shaking hands fumbled to get the key out of my purse. Unable to get the key inside the lock right away, I almost dropped my huge stack of books in my panic.

When I finally got into my car, the key nearly fell out of my hand while I threw the books onto the passenger seat. I locked the doors right away and started the ignition. My hearted pounded inside my ears until the car started. Then, my foot pushed full throttle on the gas, and off I went, gripping my steering wheel tightly as if my life depended on it.

As I drove into town and saw crowds of people, relief flooded my heart. I pulled the car over to the curb because I needed a few moments to calm down. As I sat silently in my car, I began to wonder how that hiker had seen the stranger with a knife from so far away. Where did he disappear to? How could he have vanished while I glanced back at the boulder for a mere few seconds? Could he have been an angel?

Yes, I thought to myself. He was angel sent from God to save me from some disastrous episode. How else could we have walked away from my hillside spot without being spotted by the knife-wielding stranger? I praised God and thanked him with tears as I held on to my steering wheel. What had started out as a terrifying experience transformed into a deeply spiritual moment in time for me. I still thank God to this day for having protected me that afternoon. Thank you, Mr. Angel Hiker wherever you are.

So are there angels around us today? Yes, there are many. We might not see them or recognize them, but they are there for us. We can go on with our lives never acknowledging them, and it would not make a difference. They would still work on our behalf. But, at the same time, realizing their existence can strengthen our faith and help us to appreciate God's power actively working in our lives.

3

ANGELS AS OUR GUARDIANS

Dear sisters, as women, we have an innate desire for protection—by a father, a mother, a boyfriend, a brother or by simply someone who loves us. Many of us especially yearn for a male figure to fulfill that role in our lives. Unfortunately, those protectors have fallen short at one time or another—some of them never meeting our need to shield us from the dangers and hurts of this life.

On the other hand, we may have had times when our protector came to our rescue at just the right time. As I grow older and look back at my life, I realize how little credit or appreciation I have shown to people who have helped me over the years. In fact, I know that there are people who have been there for me and have helped me at crucial times that I have completely forgotten about. To those people, I humbly apologize and encourage you with the thought that your reward is in heaven.

Without your noticing, seeing or recognizing it, God has had his guiding hand in your life—yes, through the good and bad times. He probably sent angels at key points, but you were unaware of it. Then again, you may remember traumatic times when you *felt* no angel or guiding hand in your life. We can end up writing another whole book on *why, when* and *how come,* but that is not the point of this chapter. We may never know and understand the full extent of why God intervenes at certain times and not at others. And we also need to be aware that he very much may have intervened in ways that we are not even in touch with.

The fact is that God does not send these heavenly beings randomly. Each time there seems to be a grand overall plan. As I mentioned earlier, the Bible gives numerous accounts of angels appearing to God's people, protecting his servants, saving them from harm and even death. God sends them at just the right time so that he can continue to fulfill his purposes through them. Whether it was keeping Hagar and Ishmael from dying of dehydration in the desert or shutting the mouths of hungry lions to safeguard Daniel in the lion's den for a whole night, God sent these celestial beings as keepers of his sheep.

One powerful example of angels being used as guardians occurs prior to the destruction of Sodom and Gomorrah when God sends them to assess the state of affairs of the city. When the angels arrive at the city gate, they immediately meet Lot who bows to them with his face to the ground and calls them lords (Genesis 19:1–3). He also offers them food and a place to stay. Somehow, Lot knew that these men were special, and he treated them with honor and respect. Lot tries to protect the two visitors by keeping them in his home, but the men of Sodom invade Lot's home in order to violate his guests— both young and old men from every part of the city of Sodom surround Lot's home (Genesis 19:4–11).

It is a paradox that Lot is trying to protect the two angels when, in actuality, they came to help Lot and his family before the city was destroyed. Of all the people of Sodom, it is sad that Lot is the only one who recognizes these visitors to be worthy of esteem. The eyes of all the other men in the town—both young and old— become blind not only spiritually but also physically because of the evil in their hearts. Their wickedness further convinces the angels that

Sodom had to be destroyed.

We can only speculate about Lot's wife, as her presence during the angels' stay is not mentioned in the Scriptures. In fact, it seems that she is not the one to prepare the meal for the visitors (Genesis 19:3). Unlike Sarah who prepares the meal for two angels in Genesis 18, it is Lot who bakes the bread and feeds the guests. Probably Lot's wife did not see these visitors as important, thus ignoring her duties as a "good" wife. Lot wound up doing much of the work. Again, we do not know what was going on with Lot's wife, so this is only conjecture.

Despite God's effort to save Lot and his family, Lot hesitates to leave Sodom. There is a need for urgency as the city is about to be destroyed. God sends not just one angel but two to warn them of the impending danger.

> At break of day, the angels pushed Lot to get going, "Hurry. Get your wife and two daughters out of here before it's too late and you're caught in the punishment of the city."
>
> Lot was dragging his feet. The men grabbed Lot's arm, and the arms of his wife and daughter—God was so merciful to them!—and dragged them to safety outside the city. When they had them outside, Lot was told, "Now run for your life! Don't look back! Don't stop anywhere on the plain—run for the hills or you'll be swept away." (Genesis 19:15-17, The Message)

Lot and his family were "dragging their feet." For this reason, the angels needed to grab each of their arms and force them to leave the city! These angels were extremely aggressive about saving this family from imminent destruction, doing everything possible to help them—even using force to drag them out.

Unfortunately, Lot's wife was disobedient, looking back as they ran out of the city, and, as a result, she did not make it to safety. Instead, she turned into a pillar of salt. However, the rest of the family was spared for their faithfulness.

God was merciful to Lot and his family. He is compassionate and gracious to all of us even as we struggle through doubts and hesitate to step out on faith. Sometimes God will use his celestial servants to push us in the right direction to protect us from harm. These angels are visible to even "unspiritual" people as we saw in Sodom. Other times, they can be invisible, still working great miracles. But don't worry—it will not be a measure of your spirituality whether you see them or not as we will discuss more in-depth later. These protectors are ever-present regardless if we are at our worst or at our best. That is God's great love and kindness.

4

ANGELS AS MESSENGERS

God blessed me during my high school years with a wonderful car, given to me by my father. It was a used 1980 320i BMW that I affectionately named the "Silver Bullet." I drove my car everywhere, and like a "special friend," it was a faithful car. As a college student, I continued to use it as I served in the youth ministry, driving teenagers to and from church as well as to Bible study groups. My car was also very popular among the guys at church—all of them were tremendously eager to borrow it for their special dates.

In short, the Silver Bullet became a means for helping many Christians and non-Christians in their times of need. It was a major key to my involvement with the teen ministry, because it enabled me to study the Bible and encourage many teen girls in their faith. For this reason, I believe that Satan looked for opportunities to prevent me from using my car. There were many instances where I was blocked from going to church because of "freak" accidents, car trouble or parking issues. Each time, however, God worked behind the scenes to guide me out of trouble. I believe that angels were behind many of these supernatural events.

One such incident involved a serious car accident when I was driving several teens and college students back to their homes. It was late at night, and I had just dropped off the last of the teenagers. I was stopped at a red traffic light near my dorm with two remaining college students still in the car. My car had just come out of the shop after some repairs, so I was being extra careful.

Suddenly, out of nowhere, another car appeared, speeding down my side of the road, head-on, from the opposite direction! The driver was obviously drunk, because she was completely out of control swerving back and forth from lane to lane into my side of traffic. Even as the light turned green, I remained stationary hoping that she would pass by without hitting my car. The driver, however, was coming at such high speed that it didn't matter whether I was immobile or not, and before I knew it, she managed to crash into my car with enough force to bounce me across two lanes! My car was completely smashed on the left front side. It was almost as if she had been using me for target practice with her car!

After the driver's reckless assault, she hastily drove off, not slowing down for even a moment. She seemed determined to escape the consequences of her carelessness. Her car took off down a small residential road disappearing from sight in a matter of seconds. I was speechless and frozen in the middle of the road. I dropped my head onto my steering wheel, devastated as I thought about the damage to my car. All of us were shaken, thankful though that we were not hurt, and bewildered by what had just happened.

After a quick silent prayer, I drove in the direction of the hit-and-run driver. However, my left tire was imbedded deeply into the hood of the car, so I could not go very far. So I parked on the left hand side of the road, out of the way of traffic, on the one way street.

(It's important to note that though severe, the damage was not visible from the street side of my car.) Straining to look down the road in the dark, all hope of catching the crazy driver was lost as I could detect no trace of her.

This time, I was really desperate and bowed my head and fervently began to pray. The two college girls in the back seat were discussing how crazy the drunk driver was while I quietly begged God for guidance:

God, you know that I use this car to serve you. What just happened? Now—I won't be able to find that person because my car can barely move. I need your help right now...please God...do something, so that I can find her.

As I finished my prayer, I looked up to see a man driving by me in a large car. He motioned to me in order to get my attention as he passed by. I opened my window on the passenger side to see why he was signaling to me. He quickly asked if I was looking for someone. Without thinking, I just nodded and said, "Yes." The stranger gave me some complicated directions to find the "person" that I was looking for. Although it was only a short distance away, it took us about ten minutes to get there in my malfunctioning and broken down car.

When we arrived at the location that the stranger had indicated, we clearly saw the perpetrator sitting in her car in someone's driveway—ducking out of sight in an effort to hide. Apparently, she suspected that we would come after her, so she had decided to "lie low." We didn't know what to do at that point, but the owners of the house were afraid of the stranger in their driveway and had already called the police. Within seconds of us arriving, the police came with their bright lights flashing. What incredible timing!

Evidently, there were several witnesses to my car accident as well as to the others that she caused! She had slammed into three other cars before crashing into mine. This intoxicated woman had wreaked havoc on the streets of Boston for the past thirty minutes with her uncontrolled driving. As a result, the police had received several complaints about this driver within a span of a few minutes, and they had sent three patrol cars into the neighborhood to find this public menace. The woman was arrested on the spot, hand-cuffed and taken away in one of the patrol cars.

Fortunately, with all the police reports and eye-witnesses, my car was repaired at no cost to me, and I was on the road again with a rented car from the insurance company the following day! Hours later, after the excitement had died down, my two friends and I sat in our dorm room talking about the accident. We realized that the stranger who directed me to the drunk driver must have been an angel. There was no other explanation. How could he have known— first that my car had been damaged, and second such specifics about the person I was looking for? Wow, what a night!

The word *angel* actually means "messenger." In biblical accounts, God used these heavenly beings to communicate his will, his warning and his direction as well as helpful information. Whether it was to impart the news of Jesus' birth to the shepherds in the field or to reveal his plan to Mary about her and Elizabeth's pregnancies, his messengers were a crucial part of God's design and purposes. Joseph and Mary's encounters with angels kept them and baby Jesus safe throughout all their challenges. In fact, every time danger would draw near them, an angel was there to warn them:

> After Jesus was born in Bethlehem in Judea, during the time of King Herod, Magi from the east came to Jerusalem and asked, "Where is the one who has been born king of the Jews? We saw his star in the east and have come to worship him."
>
> When King Herod heard this he was disturbed, and all Jerusalem with him.
>
> When they had gone, an angel of the Lord appeared

to Joseph in a dream. "Get up," he said, "take the child
and his mother and escape to Egypt. Stay there until I tell
you, for Herod is going to search for the child to kill him."

So he got up, took the child and his mother during the
night and left for Egypt. (Matthew 2:1-3, 13-14)

Bethlehem was a town five miles (eight kilometers) outside of
Jerusalem, so for the Magi to stop in Jerusalem on their way to
Bethlehem to get directions would have been a very common practice for travelers during those days. King Herod, however, was greatly disturbed by their visit. He was an Idumaenean from the land of
Edom. His reign lasted from 37 BC to 4 BC.[3] Any new "king" would
threaten his standing as the existing ruler and, therefore, had to be
destroyed. Consequently, King Herod was determined to find Jesus
and kill him in order to remove this threat to his throne.

The actual birth of Christ is calculated to have been in 4 BC or 3
BC coinciding with the last years of King Herod's reign, which ended
shortly after Jesus' birth. (The best guess for his actual birth is sometime in September, 3 BC.)[4] Before his death and the conclusion of his
reign, Herod ensured a legacy of infamy by the atrocity of murder-
ing all the little boys in Bethlehem who were two years old or
younger. It was right before the time of this murderous edict that
God sent an angel to Joseph warning him to leave Bethlehem.

From the very moment that Jesus was conceived, God used
angels to convey his will to Joseph and Mary. From making sure that
Joseph did not divorce Mary to telling him just the right time to safely leave Bethlehem, God's messengers were present to guide Joseph
and Mary's steps. Angels also warned the Magi in a dream not to go
back to Herod. So instead of reporting back the location of the baby,
the Magi traveled a different road home, thwarting the king's initial
plan.

In the same way, it is possible that many of you have spoken to angels. They may have appeared in your dreams as people you knew or thought you knew. They might have told you to do something that was important for your future. You might have heard a voice speaking to you when you were all alone, driving in a car or sitting at home. This is what happened to my husband as a young minister in San Francisco.

After an evening Bible study in Walnut Creek, Frank was returning home through a tunnel not far from the Bay Bridge. He was extremely tired, and without realizing it, he fell asleep behind the wheel. Out of the blue, he heard a loud voice yell out his name, "Frank, wake up!" He woke up, but no one was there! Needless to say, he stayed awake for the rest of the drive home.

The truth is that God has not changed his technique of communicating to his children. Believe it or not, we live in spiritually active times! God is working just as powerfully now as he did in biblical times. We just need to decide to open up our spiritual eyes and hearts so that we can see God working. Sadly, our day-to-day schedule filled with appointments, errands, housecleaning, children, work, school and church responsibilities, keeps many of us from recognizing God's active hand working around us. We dismiss miracles as a twist of fate. We write off answered prayers as mere luck. We disregard God's interventions and call them coincidences.

That certain gentleman who helped you the other day was simply a "nice man." The stranger who encouraged you a few months ago with thoughtful words was just a "kind person." Even the woman who found your lost child in the mall was merely a "sweet lady."

Obviously, these statements could all be true, but we cannot dismiss all such happenings as chance or happenstance. That would mean that God is a weak and uninvolved Father in our lives. Wouldn't it make more sense that every one of those instances was God's hand working to direct and assist us in our time of need —whether by moving another person's heart or by intervening through angels?

Many of us want proof—hardcore, visible evidence. If we see that sparkle, glow of light or that magical shimmer, then we might believe. However, I imagine that if God did that to his people, most of them would have run away in fear instead of listening to the messenger! Look what happened to Moses when he saw the burning bush, which was probably one of the most dramatic of God's manifestations. Moses was afraid—and he was the son of a Pharaoh!

In reality, God's people were often humble and simple people, who needed guidance, not pomp and show in the way we might expect. That happens in the movies, but not always in real life! As a matter of fact, God works in very ordinary situations with common looking people. Besides, God is not all about being a show off.

Interestingly, one of the first angels cited in the Bible appears to Hagar, an Egyptian maidservant. She was not a hero of faith nor was she someone who did something amazing. To a certain extent, she was a victim of an unfortunate circumstance. She was asked to sleep with her master in order to have a child and becomes prideful when she conceives. The Bible says that after Hagar became pregnant, she despised Sarah (Genesis16:4).

As a result, Sarah complained to her husband, Abraham, who told her to do what she wanted with her servant girl. She treated Hagar harshly, causing her to run away (Genesis 16:5–6). While she was fleeing from Sarah, an angel appeared and told Hagar to go home and submit to her mistress.

God had a purpose for Hagar, but it was not an easy path. The servant girl was probably heading home towards Egypt, as far away from Sarah as possible. In her distress, an angel appears to her and promises to increase her descendants to be too numerous to count. The maidservant is obedient to the vision and returns to her mistress.

Sometimes the righteous paths are the most difficult ones. In this case, Hagar had to return and face a difficult relationship, but it might have been vital to her survival. A pregnant woman walking alone in the desert had little chance to survive. But after she returned, there seems to be no record of further harsh treatment. She submitted to God and surrendered her future.

Angels do not necessarily bring good news nor do they lead his people into the easiest paths. The path or the purpose God might lead us to, may not make sense at the time. But when his servants listen to his message, as Hagar did, his glory is revealed in their lives. In Hagar's case, her son became the father of a nation!

5

ANGELIC INTERVENTION

The Bible is full of stories where angels intervene at key times. In one story, an angel completely blocks a man named Balaam from cursing God's people—a very evil act in the sight of the Lord. Balaam falls into the temptation of prestige and money, leading him to pursue his wicked path. Balaam is not an Israelite, but appears to be some kind of sorcerer or spiritualist who is able to call upon different gods.[5] God speaks directly to Balaam. It is interesting how God communicates directly to a man who is not one of his servants.

> And God came to Balaam and said, "Who are these men with you?" And Balaam said to God, "Balak the son of Zippor, king of Moab, has sent to me saying, 'Behold, a people has come out of Egypt, and it covers the face of the earth; now come, curse them for me; perhaps I shall be able to fight against them and drive them out.'" God said to Balaam, "You shall not go with them; you shall not curse the people, for they are blessed." (Numbers 22:9-12, RSV)

God specifically prohibits Balaam from going with the Moabites. He intercedes to protect the Israelites and commands Balaam not to curse the people because they are blessed. After God speaks to him, Balaam goes back to the princes of Moab and refuses to do their bidding. Despite his efforts to decline their appeal, Balaam is approached again, but this time by more honorable and numerous princes than before.

The world always offers many "opportunities" that can be destructive. In this case, Balaam was presented with an offer that may have set him up well for life, but was damaging to the Israelites. Balaam was not an Israelite, but he must have heard about the God of the Israelites and all his incredible miracles. This could have been an occasion for him to change and to believe, like Ruth who was a Moabitess. But at this point in the narrative he does not take that step of faith. God even speaks to him directly, which is more than he does for other unbelievers in the Old Testament, yet Balaam continues in his corrupt ways.

God shows his love for his people throughout this event, because he is working on their behalf while they know nothing about what is going on. Balak, the king of Moab, wanted to hurt God's people. He was afraid of them and wanted to curse them before they destroyed him with their powerful God. So Balaam is offered the opportunity of a lifetime—treasures and prominence—if he will simply put a curse on the Israelites. This unfolding story shows how God is watching over his people and is working even when they are totally unaware.

When God speaks to Balaam, it was enough to make him refuse to curse the Israelites.

> But Balaam answered them, "Even if Balak gave me his palace filled with silver and gold, I could not do anything great or small to go beyond the command of the LORD my

God. Now stay here tonight as the others did, and I will find out what else the LORD will tell me." (Numbers 22:18-19)

Here Balaam makes a grandiose claim that he would not accept even the king's palace in exchange for following through with their request. Yet, Balaam is clearly tempted, because he does not send the men on their way. Instead, he asks them to stay with him that night. Why would he ask them to remain with him if he had been resolute in his decision? God had made his will clear to Balaam. Nonetheless, Balaam possibly wanted room for compromise, so that he could get a little bit out of this deal.

Satan wants to destroy God's people, meaning you and me. He will use whatever opportunity he can to make sure that we are torn down by others. Even as you read these words, Satan has a scheme to use people at work, at school or in your neighborhood to hurt you. But God is faithful. He is also working in their lives, yes, in the lives of those who plan to hurt you, so that they will not be able to carry out their plans. He will intervene, using circumstances, dreams or even angels to prevent them from their destructive path. While, at other times, he allows them to follow through with their plans, to help us become stronger and more faithful.

Sadly, Balaam makes the wrong decision. God had said he could go with the men, but that he was to speak only God's words. Although he goes with the men, apparently his motives are not pure because God was angry with him. God uses a donkey and an angel to block him. But Balaam is determined, even to the point of beating his faithful donkey (Numbers 22:21–23):

Then the LORD opened the donkey's mouth, and she said to Balaam, "What have I done to you to make you beat me these three times?"

Balaam answered the donkey, "You have made a fool

of me! If I had a sword in my hand, I would kill you right now."

The donkey said to Balaam, "Am I not your own donkey, which you have ridden, to this day? Have I been in the habit of doing this to you?"

"No," he said.

Then the LORD opened Balaam's eyes, and he saw the angel of the Lord standing in the road with his sword drawn. So he bowed low and fell facedown. (Numbers 22:28 - 31)

Balaam was extremely angry with the donkey, because he wanted to follow the princes of Moab, but his donkey was misbehaving. The donkey's behavior likely caused a stir among the princes, embarrassing Balaam in front all the royalty. In contrast, the princes were probably riding on fine steeds with expensive saddles and adornment, walking with grace and elegance. Meanwhile, Balaam was struggling to control his old donkey, which jumps into a field, presses Balaam's foot against a wall and lies down on the ground. How awkward from Balaam's perspective! But God must have been shaking his head from side to side as Balaam beat the poor creature at every step.

If all this was not enough, Balaam starts talking to his donkey! What a sight this must have been! This scene was absolutely ludicrous. Meanwhile, the princes of Moab might have been watching him and wondering if they had made a mistake about asking him for help. *Is this man really able to help the king? Does he have the power to curse a nation? Why is he talking to his donkey? Should the king really use this "spiritual" man?*

God loves us very much. Though he sent an angel to destroy Balaam, he loved Balaam enough to give him a chance not to be destroyed by enabling his donkey to speak to him. Yet, Balaam was stubborn. He was blinded by his unyielding attitude and did not see the miracle of God in his life. Even as his donkey spoke, he was not terrified but accepted it as being normal! What should have opened his eyes to God's guidance only exasperated him more. In fact, Balaam tells his donkey that he would kill him if he had a sword.

Imagine how many instances in our lives that God intervened with his angels. He might have used an animal, an unexpected event, or even a natural phenomenon like a snowstorm or hurricane to protect us. We will never know, until we get to heaven, how many times God used his angels to block and to prevent us from getting hurt or killed before our time. If we could see a movie about our lives and rewind it to certain key times, we would marvel at the great love God has for us.

So don't be so fast to come to the conclusion that God never helped you or that he doesn't love you enough to rescue you. He has been working invisibly as well as visibly to intervene. He is not an uninvolved Father but one that is completely involved in every aspect of your life! So do not be afraid:

> "Don't be afraid," the prophet answered. "Those who are with us are more than those who are with them."
> (2 Kings 6:16)

On September 11, 2001, America faced a terrorist attack that rocked the lives of every American. Two commercial planes were used as missiles to take down the World Trade Center in New York City. Being a native-born New Yorker, the attacks shook me to the core. One of my friend's acquaintances, a Christian working inside the second building to be hit, had left her office together with some other co-workers because of an announcement to evacuate. This directive had been given as soon as the first building was struck. Apparently, there was a great deal of confusion and fear as the workers began descending the emergency stairs. No one inside either of the buildings had any idea what was happening.

After a few minutes, there was a subsequent announcement saying that the second tower was not hit, so all workers needed to report back to their offices. This one woman, however, felt like something was wrong. As her co-workers began getting into the elevator to return to their office, she started to plead with them to leave the building with her. They began to laugh at her "paranoia" and tried to coax her to get into the elevator. When she refused, they boarded the elevator without her. In sickening synchronism, the second plane hit the tower just as the elevator doors shut. She heard the elevator cables sever inside the shaft and her friends plummet, screaming to their deaths.

The cries of distress made her immediately pass out, but as she lost consciousness, she saw two hands scoop her up. When she awoke, she was outside the tower. Someone had carried her down the stairs—over fifty flights!

There have been a myriad of times that God has taken care of us and prevented accidents, death and tragedy. Though he doesn't block or stop every one of our painful experiences, he inhibits and sometimes stops others. As I said earlier, I don't know why God chooses some and not others, but, dear sisters, be assured that he is always watching over each one of us.

He uses his angels to speak to our hearts. Other times, his angels help us make the right decision through a dream or an encounter with a stranger. Then, there are times when an angel will intervene and carry us in his arms to safety or move someone else to when we cannot go ourselves.

> I lift up my eyes to the hills—
>> where does my help come from?
> My help comes from the LORD,
>> the Maker of heaven and earth.

He will not let your foot slip—
    he who watches over you will not slumber;
indeed, he who watches over Israel
    will neither slumber nor sleep.

The LORD watches over you—
    the LORD is your shade at your right hand;
the sun will not harm you by day,
    nor the moon by night.

The LORD will keep you from all harm—
    he will watch over your life;
the LORD will watch over your coming and going
    both now and forevermore. (Psalm 121)

Truly, angels are amazing beings who have the ability to warn, to block, to save and to relay good news. Their works are ever present around us each day of our lives. Without them, very crucial events would not have been possible. God knew what he was doing when he created these heavenly beings. Their charge to minister to different people is vital to God's plan around us. We are blessed to be taken care of by such powerful beings of light.

STUDY QUESTIONS

Angels: Are They Truly Around Me?

1. There are different kinds of angels or celestial beings mentioned in the Bible. Go back and read some of the scripture references from Isaiah 6, Hebrews 1 and 2, and Revelation 4. Compare and write down the differences between the various heavenly beings. Pray to see some insights into these spiritual beings.

2. Angels still exist today, ministering to those who will inherit

salvation (Hebrews 1:14). Think back at some moment in your life in which there seemed to be no logical explanation for something that occurred. If you cannot remember anything in particular, pray about being more alert in recognizing how God helps you through challenging times.

3. In Genesis 19, God used two angels to protect Lot and his family from being destroyed along with Sodom and Gomorrah. Go back and read that chapter. Try to imagine how Lot felt during that time in his life.

   a. How can we stay pure like Lot around our worldly friends?

   b. Have you been a great example around people who have a different standard of morals from you?

   c. Do they sway you, or do you influence them more?

4. The word angel means "messenger." If God were to send you a message from an angel, what do you think that he would tell you? Would he send good news or would he warn you about your life?

   a. Make a decision to pray more about important decisions in your life.

   b. What crucial choices are before you right now? Have you prayed for guidance?

   c. If you haven't prayed much about the difficult options in your life, allow prayer to be a part of those choices.

5. In the last section of the chapter on angels, we saw how God opened the eyes of a donkey to block Balaam from a path of destruction. He was asked by the princes of Moab to curse Israel. God did not want him to curse his people because they were a blessed nation. In the same way, we are a blessed nation. Pray to renew your confidence that God is always watching over you, and thank him during the next week for all the ways he has been guiding your life.

6. As we read about Balaam, we see that he allowed temptation to

override his judgment. We must be careful not to become like Balaam. How has God made sure that you do not go astray?

a. If you did go on the wrong path for a while in your life, how did you see God working to lead you back to him?

b. Do you find yourself fighting God's will in your life right now?

c. If you find it difficult to walk on the right path, make sure that you trust and ask other Christians to pray with you and for you.

Prayer

WHY DO IT WHEN GOD ALREADY KNOWS?

"I will answer them before they even call to me. While they are still talking about their needs, I will go ahead and answer their prayers!"

Isaiah 65:24 (NLT)

1
WHY WE NEED TO PRAY

I have been a Christian for twenty-seven years now. As I look back at my walk with the Lord, I see many victories and many disappointments. Did I pray during the victorious times? Yes. Did I pray during the tough times? Yes. God answered all my prayers *his way* and not my way. Somehow, though, God would "twist" his "no" to become a "yes" just to make sure that I knew that he did hear me.

For instance, I prayed for a third child for many years, but I was not able to have one because of health problems. I believed that God had given me a "no" answer for almost ten years! Then, just when I was ready to give up, I was pregnant with my third child, Mimi! All of us who have been Christians for a number of years have experienced similar victories and disappointments in prayer. Yet, we keep on praying—hoping, believing, expecting and trusting. Why? Because we have faith that somehow God will work out his plans in response to our prayers.

One Sunday I listened to a sermon in which the preacher shared about a father and a daughter. The daughter had been eyeing some pretty plastic pearls in a store and wanted them very badly. She begged her father to buy her the pearls, but her father told her no.

At night as the father was putting his little girl to bed; he asked her, "Do you know that your daddy loves you very much?"

"Yes," the girl replied.

"Do you love your daddy?" he asked her.

"Yes, of course, Daddy," she replied.

A few days later, the girl still could not get those pearls out of her mind. Her birthday was coming up, so she decided to ask her parents for them again. This time they did not say "no" or "yes." On her birthday, she received those much desired pearls from her parents. She was so happy that night.

At night during her bedtime, as her father was tucking her into bed, he said, "Honey, I love you very much. Do you know that?"

"Yes, Daddy, I do," she replied.

"If you really love me, honey, then give me your pearls," pleaded the father.

The girl looked at her father with surprised eyes. She saw that her father was serious. Selfishly, the little girl clutched onto her beloved new pearls.

The next night, her father came to tuck in his daughter again. He said the same thing: "If you really love me, then give me your pearls."

The daughter was sad; she was unable to give up her pearls once again.

The third night came, and the father was getting ready to ask his daughter the same question. Before the father asked her, however, the little girl handed her father the pearls with big tear-filled eyes and said, "I love you Daddy."

After taking the pearls away from her and putting them gently into his pocket, he said, "I love you too."

Immediately afterwards, the father smiled and took out a beautiful box from his other pocket. He handed it to his daughter who was surprised by what she saw. She slowly opened the box only to see a real pearl necklace within the box! In fact, the father had bought the real ones for her birthday but was waiting for his daughter to focus on what was most important—which was their relationship. The father brought the box with him every night just waiting for his daughter to make the right choice, to trust that he had her best in mind!

Despite all our seemingly unanswered prayers, God has been listening to every word uttered by our lips. And even all our reflections and longings that were never communicated are known to him. In reality, our prayers are not empty words that get lost on the way to heaven. God has heard our thoughts and desires even before we expressed them in prayer. There are special places in his heart for each of our prayers—even for the ones we have long forgotten. Believe it or not, our requests to God have great power to move heaven and earth. Prayers are not only heard by God, but have a mighty impact.

> Another angel, who had a golden censer, came and stood at the altar. He was given much incense to offer, with the prayers of all the saints, on the golden altar before the throne. The smoke of the incense, together with the prayers of the saints, went up before God from the angel's hand. Then the angel took the censer, filled it with fire from the altar, and hurled it on the earth; and there came peals of thunder, rumblings, flashes of lightning and an earthquake. (Revelation 8:3-5)

After reading this passage, you can imagine what happens when the prayers of the saints, that is, Christians, reach up into heaven. An angel carries them up to God according to the scripture. There is an angel assigned to hold your prayers and bring them to God! Out of *your* prayers come fires, peals of thunder, rumblings and flashes of lightning and even an earthquake. That is quite a powerful product of prayer! The words we whisper in the silence of our bedrooms while kneeling beside our bed are not the same in heaven. In fact, those hushed and unspoken reverberations of the heart result in loud quakes and rumblings—and yes, fire and lightning! Every prayer request has a deep effect on God's heavenly world. How could God ignore such a ruckus?

Imagine if the whole church prayed and brought up the same request over and over again. The power and energy that echoes into the heavens must be incredible. There is a golden altar for your prayers as well as for all the saints. There are angels who tend to your specific prayers. Of course, how they get answered is all up to God. But each of your prayers is placed in a magnificent and splendid part of the heavenly kingdom—a golden altar before the throne of God.

> When he took the scroll, the four living creatures and the twenty-four elders bowed down before the Lamb. Each one of them had a harp and golden bowls full of incense, which are the prayers of God's holy people. (Revelation 5:8, NCV)

Dear sisters, could you have ever imagined all of this going on from one prayer or a series of prayers? Our prayers are transformed into golden bowls of incense. Your special incense fills God's throne with its wonderful aroma. When we ladies go to the spa, there is often a bowl of incense that is placed in the room to help us relax and enjoy the ambiance. To God, our prayers fill his heavenly kingdom with a rich perfume, and every prayer is precious—an offering just like the one made by the priests in the Old Testament and the same offering made by the Magi to welcome Jesus into the world. It is worship at its deepest.

Do you have to be an important person to be heard? Do you have to be perfect for God to answer, "Yes"? No, you can just be you, and God will hear every word. God will listen to a child's words in just the same way he would to you. There is no difference. Even if you may *feel* insignificant, your prayers have great influence. Satan wants us to believe that our prayers are meaningless or ineffective. Why would God place our prayers in golden bowls if they were not important? He could have put them into plain wooden bowls, but, instead, the elders and other angelic beings are holding your prayers in bowls made of the most precious mineral found on earth.

You see, it is easy to lose sight of the importance of your prayers. God gives you the power of influence—the ability to influence the King of kings and the Lord of lords—to work on your behalf. Influence is different from muscle power. Influence is causing an effect without using physical force. God gives you the power to sway him, to move him and to compel him with your words. How marvelous is that?

One of my favorite movies is *My Big Fat Greek Wedding*. There is a line in the movie when the daughter is complaining about her father to her mother.

Toula Portokalos says, "Ma, Dad is so stubborn. What he says goes. 'Ah, the man is the head of the house!'"

Then her mother, Maria Portokalos, replies, "Let me tell you something, Toula. The man is the head, but the woman is the neck. And she can turn the head any way she wants."

Of course, Maria's answer indicates more than just a little bit of relational manipulation. But in a humorous way, it reminds us of the power our requests can have.

Your influence through prayer is more powerful than you can ever dream. Have you lost sight of the awe-inspiring influence of your prayers? Have you forgotten how much power God has placed in your hands through your ability to pray? No matter what you may feel at a certain time, God loves you and he works on your behalf all the time. He is especially attentive to those who are in need or in trouble:

> God gives a hand to those down on their luck,
> gives a fresh start to those ready to quit.
> All eyes are on you, expectant;
> you give them their meals on time.
> Generous to a fault,
> you lavish your favor on all creatures.
> Everything God does is right—
> the trademark on all his works is love.
> God's there, listening for all who pray,
> for all who pray and mean it.
> He does what's best for those who fear him—
> hears them call out, and saves them.
> (Psalm 145:14-19, The Message)

And when your prayers reach up to him, he does what is best for you, knowing what you desire. He hears and saves those of you who are hurting. God is generous. He will lavish his favor on you. He will do what is right. He will be there for you because he is your Father in heaven. The Message translation of this scripture even says that God is "generous to a fault"!

Sisters, are you feeling lonely? Are you feeling afraid? Is life going too fast for you, and you do not know what to do? Are you in a situation in which you are being treated unfairly? Have the tides of grief washed over you? God is always there—ready to listen, prepared to calm your heart and eager to mend the hurt inside of you.

During the darkest times in the Bible, it was the prayers of faithful men and women that allowed God to work despite the opposition and difficulties of the time. I am sure that all of them prayed for months, and even years, to be released from the oppression of the moment, but God had a different timing in mind. Yet, these men and women of faith did not let go of their faith but clung to their hope in their God and continued to pray no matter what the outcome was. When they prayed, they released their anxieties, fears and worries, handing them over to the One who could take care of them. Paul says,

> Don't worry about anything; instead, pray about every-thing. Tell God what you need, and thank him for all he has done. Then you will experience God's peace, which exceeds anything we can understand. His peace will guard your hearts and minds as you live in Christ Jesus. (Philippians 4:6-7, NLT)

Through prayer, a peace that surpasses all understanding will guard your heart and mind. It will protect us from Satan's influence, which can make us doubt and even sin. Remember Jesus before the cross? He begged his disciples to pray with him even though they were exhausted and sleepy. He found them sleeping after his prayer, and so he woke them up. He asked them to pray with him a second time so they would not fall into temptation (Matthew 26:40–41). But instead of praying, all the disciples went back to sleep. No won-der they ended up betraying Jesus at such a crucial time.

As a human being, even Jesus needed prayer for strength. His human energy and desire were not strong enough to overcome the evil one, even though he was the Son of God. Jesus wanted to pray *with* his disciples, not all alone. Jesus understood something about prayer that his disciples didn't. He tapped into the supernatural—the spiritual power that had all supremacy and rule in this world. That was why Jesus did not sin, especially on the cross where the tempta-tion was overpowering. It kept him bonded and connected to his Father. Prayer is all about power through connection—connection to the greatest power in existence—to our Lord and Savior. The more we connect, the more God can accomplish through us.

For this reason, prayer is all about relationship—a relationship with the Creator. If we ask, he can even make a mountain throw itself into the sea (Matthew 21:21). He wants us to rely on him. A relationship cannot be built on one side alone. It requires both parties taking the initiative to draw close to one another. God has done so much in order to have a relationship with us. He used every possible measure to lovingly commune with us whether through his prophets or through sending his Son.

And since God is a relational being, He wants us to make an effort to be close to him too! God wants to bless our lives through prayer. He wants to give us more than we ask or imagine. But the little girl inside of us holds onto the "plastic pearls" because we do not trust that God has something better in store for our lives.

Deep prayer begins with complete dependence on God through faith. Whether we pray at church or at mealtimes or during our personal times with God, God can work through even the tiniest prayers. The length or the words do not matter to God. Likewise, when my young daughter writes me short notes to tell me she loves me, or when she tells me with long drawn out words that she loves me, I appreciate both, and more than anything, I hear her heart.

Recently, I was looking through my prayer journals and found a list of prayers from years ago that I had completely forgotten about. To my surprise, I saw that God had answered almost every prayer! And I am sure with the ones that did not seem to be answered in the affirmative, he did what was best.

What I saw was that even though I may forget to keep praying about certain things, God never forgets what he heard. And though it may be years later, he keeps working on my prayers.

2

DESPERATE TIMES CALL FOR DESPERATE MEASURES

I was diagnosed with Lupus sometime in 1990, which was a year after the birth of my second child. Working for the church along with having a two-year-old and a newborn did not allow for me to rest and recover properly. My body was already susceptible to the disease since my mother was a genetic carrier. With my health deteriorating during those months, my father convinced me to go to the hospital and get tested for Lupus (SLE). Despite my mother being ill with the disease, I never imagined that I would face the same challenge, because I had been a healthy person until then.

Yet, in order to appease my father, I went to the hospital to get tested for the disease. Much to my shock, the doctor confirmed my condition and relayed the alarming news to me.

In the subsequent months, shock and denial kept me immobilized. My reluctance to get medical attention right away caused my condition to worsen very quickly. By 1991, I could not even get out of bed. I had hair loss, migraines, vomiting, joint pains, lesions all over my body and weight loss. The lupus found its way into my liver. I was in a desperate situation. We did not have enough money to pay for long-term hospitalization, so I remained at home completely bedridden. Thankfully, my aunt came to take care of my children and me during that time.

By 1992, I could not even sit up in bed to read my Bible. I spent hours in bed praying for others as well as for my healing. I struggled with accepting my condition. I also battled with guilt as I could not take care of my children or my husband. During those days when my disease took an aggressive course in my life, I learned to rely on God through prayer. Frank and I became so desperate that we would spend many hours in prayer. Here I was at twenty-seven years old looking at the possibility of death. With each passing month, we would hold on to the hope that I would feel better if I kept resting.

The Bible is full of true stories of people who suffered hard times, endured extreme persecution and experienced severe crises. One of the prophets that I enjoy reading about the most is Elijah. Because the king and the people of God had turned away from the Lord, Elijah prayed for there to be a famine in the land. In fact, he prayed for no rain. During the famine, he lived in seclusion and was fed by ravens and drank water from a brook. Eventually, the brook dried up. And God asked him to go to Zarephath of Sidon.

> Elijah was a man just like us. He prayed earnestly that it would not rain, and it did not rain on the land for three and a half years. Again he prayed, and the heavens gave rain, and the earth produced its crops. (James 5:17-18)

It is quite encouraging to know that Elijah was a man just like us. He was not a special magician or a "superman," He was merely a man who loved the Lord and prayed earnestly for the Israelites and their king. Israel had gone completely astray from God's laws. For this reason, Elijah had to pray desperate prayers to God. He asked God for a famine.

Often, our prayers get more fervent with the increased difficulty of a situation. Your son or daughter might have been diagnosed with a serious illness. For this reason, you are desperate in prayer. Your husband might have gotten laid off from his job and, as it was, you were already living from paycheck to paycheck. One of your parents might be dying of cancer. Or maybe you are on the brink of divorce and cannot bear the thought. These kinds of desperate moments bring us to our knees more than anything else.

Sadly, during the year when my sickness was getting serious, one of our closest friends and heroes of faith passed away with pneumonia. His name was George Gurganus, and he was the founding missionary of our church in Tokyo. On top of that, we were also under great scrutiny in our job since we were not able to perform adequately in our full-time ministry role. Needless to say, my life was in the pits. I felt like God was asking me to win a marathon after getting both my legs amputated! Elijah was also in a very desperate situation:

> Some time later the brook dried up because there had been no rain in the land. Then the word of the LORD came to him: "Go at once to Zarephath of Sidon and stay there. I have commanded a widow in that place to supply you with food." So he went to Zarephath. When he came to the town gate, a widow was there gathering sticks. He called to her and asked, "Would you bring me a little water in a jar so I may have a drink?" As she was going to get it, he called, "And bring me, please, a piece of bread."
>
> "As surely as the LORD your God lives," she replied, "I don't have any bread—only a handful of flour in a jar and a little oil in a jug. I am gathering a few sticks to take home and make a meal for myself and my son, that we may eat it—and die." (1 Kings 17:7-12)

Elijah was living at a time of famine. His only source of water was a brook. Imagine the day that the brook finally dried up. Elijah saw it coming as he watched the waters slowly dry out. Little trickles were coming down for a while until the stream became only wet dirt. What had been a desperate situation seemed to get even worse. This time, it was affecting his personal life and not just the people of Israel. Consequently, God led him to a widow in Zarephath who worshiped the Lord. She, too, was hungry and was preparing to die. It took a lot of faith on Elijah's part to ask a widow and her dying son for food.

Maybe you have never prayed a prayer like Elijah, asking for a famine or for some incredible trial so that the people you love would become Christians. Elijah was a zealous man of God, whose commitment challenges our hearts. Elijah walked a path of faith. He believed that God would work through his prayers. For this reason, Elijah reassured the widow and told her not to be afraid. He asked her to first make him a small cake of bread, then to make some for her and her son afterwards. It was a test for the widow.

It took a lot of faith on the part of the widow to trust the words of Elijah. She listened to what he had to say and did as he asked. God blessed her faith as a result. She saw that the God of Israel was truly as powerful as Elijah had said. She had to first let go of what she desired and then believe. After that, God was able to work powerfully in her life and keep her and her son alive. Elijah's faith alone was not enough for the moment. The widow was also expected to have the same level of faith!

God expects us to have faith, even in hopeless times. I felt God calling me to believe despite my situation. So Frank and I decided during the Thanksgiving holiday of 1992 to have faith and to pray like never before. The first miracle came through a phone call from our dear friends, John and Karen Louis. They were leading a church in Singapore at the time. (They are presently still in Singapore leading the same church.) They called us concerning a doctor who claimed to be able to cure terminal diseases using a strict regimen of natural foods, vitamins and cleansings. He was based in New York City, which happened to be my hometown. A burst of hope poured into my heart as I was able to contact the doctor and get an appointment with him. I praise God for using John and Karen to help me get on the road to recovery.

I was pronounced clinically cured in 1995, three years later! It was, however, not until the Christians around the world prayed and fasted for me that I made progress in my health. In fact, I improved only a little bit the first year and a half. When many brothers and sisters around the world took the initiative to pray and fast for me, true progress was made. My recovery was completely carried by the prayers of all the saints as God answered those prayers and healed me.

The events of 1992 did not end with just an answer to my illness.

> Some time later the son of the woman who owned the house became ill. He grew worse and worse, and finally stopped breathing. She said to Elijah, "What do you have against me, man of God? Did you come to remind me of my sin and kill my son?" (1 Kings 17:17-18)

Just like the widow of Zarephath says in the scripture above, I was reminded of my sin: lack of faith and trust in God. Though the widow's sin is not specified in the scripture, she was probably a former Baal worshiper. The town of Zarephath was on the Mediterranean coast between Tyre and Sidon, the home of Jezebel and the heart of Baal and Asherah worship.[1] With such beliefs prevalent in the area, we can speculate that the widow had fallen back into idol worship after the death of her husband. With the difficulties resulting from the famine and, later, receiving Elijah's aid, she was probably able to restore her faith in the true Lord. Who knows? The Bible is silent on this, so we can only conjecture what her sin was. Yet, even at this time, God's grace was alive to show her how much he loved her.

In the same way, the death of the founder of our church, George, was a big blow to my faith as he was like a father to me and also Frank's mentor and best friend. It made both of us feel all alone in our work as missionaries. Our brook had dried up, and even as we tried to recover in our faith, we still felt the challenge of our work.

> The LORD heard Elijah's cry, and the boy's life returned to him, and he lived. Elijah picked up the child and carried him down from the room into the house. He gave him to

his mother and said, "Look, your son is alive!"

Then the woman said to Elijah, "Now I know that you are a man of God and that the word of the LORD from your mouth is the truth." (1 Kings 17:22-24)

With the death of the widow's son, Elijah cried out in prayer to the Lord. It took a frantic prayer from Elijah to restore this woman's faith! Who would not become alarmed in the face of death, especially that of a child? The Lord heard Elijah's cry. In raising her son from the dead, Elijah showed the widow that he was truly a man of God. The prophet had no magic or special powers—though it may appear so. No, it was God who was at work to raise the boy from the dead. No matter how bleak the situation seemed, Elijah gave his best in crying out to the Lord.

Of course, we prayed for George's family after his death. And, no, George did not rise from the dead, but he rose to be with his Lord in heaven. He is there today waiting to meet us again. But my faith needed to rise from the dead after all the difficulties I had faced. I was like the widow. I had seen great miracles, but still lacked faith.

Soon afterwards, Frank and I decided to devote ourselves to another time of desperate prayers. We went away to the mountains, studied our Bibles and prayed. We studied out the heroes of faith and were inspired by their strength and determination through adversity and seemingly insurmountable obstacles. Each problem that these men and women of God faced was resolved through prayer. And every time, God made the impossible happen. With our own hearts inspired, we taught a Bible study series on the heroes of faith to the whole church.

Sisters, remember that Elijah was a normal person just like each one of us. During desperate times, he prayed faithful prayers which God answered.

Another woman in the Old Testament named Hannah was a typical woman wanting a child. After fervent prayer, she became the mother of Samuel the prophet.

Esther was from a humble background like many of us, but prayed to God so that she could save her people. The king listened to her as a result, and she was able to save her people!

It is never too late to get down on our knees and begin to pray radical prayers for God. Whether it is for our own faith to revive or to help others to believe in him, faith is the key to making God's power complete. Let us decide to put real faith back into our prayer lives so that God can work in mighty ways:

> If any of you lacks wisdom, he should ask God, who gives generously to all without finding fault, and it will be given to him. But when he asks, he must believe and not doubt, because he who doubts is like a wave of the sea, blown and tossed by the wind. That man should not think he will receive anything from the Lord; he is a double-minded man, unstable in all he does. (James 1:5-8)

3

DON'T GIVE UP PRAYING

How prayer works is truly a mystery. But it works! Sometimes, we can pray about the most insignificant things and get a quick answer. Other times, we can pray several times on our knees, begging God for an answer, but there seems to be no response. No matter what the outcome may be, God does not want us to give up. We understand this concept in our minds, but our hearts do not always follow. Whether it works the way we want or not, God doesn't want us to stop praying.

> Then Jesus told his disciples a parable to show them that they should always pray and not give up. He said: "In

157

a certain town there was a judge who neither feared God nor cared about men. And there was a widow in that town who kept coming to him with the plea; 'Grant me justice against my adversary.'

"For some time he refused. But finally he said to himself, 'Even though I don't fear God or care about men, yet because this widow keeps bothering me, I will see that she gets justice, so that she won't eventually wear me out with her coming!'"

And the Lord said, "Listen to what the unjust judge says. And will not God bring about justice for his chosen ones, who cry out to him day and night? Will he keep putting them off? I tell you, he will see that they get justice, and quickly. However, when the Son of Man comes, will he find faith on the earth?" (Luke 18:1-8)

In our church in Tokyo, there was a couple who gave birth to a baby boy named Yuuki, which means "courage." The doctors did not think that he was going to survive his first week of life, but they were wrong. Yuuki was truly a little boy of courage. Many of the members in our church fasted and prayed for him to live. Not only did Yuuki survive the first week, but he lived until he was nine years old! His disease was incurable, but God gave us a nine-year miracle. His life inspired the whole church. I salute you, Yuuki, for your courage to fight for those nine difficult years.

Another woman in the church found out that she was in her last stage of stomach cancer. She was too afraid to go to the doctor, so she waited until it was too late. By the time she was diagnosed, she was in the fourth stage of cancer. Her husband was extremely desperate to save her life. So he told everyone at church that if their prayers worked, he would become a Christian. The church dedicated itself to fervently praying for this woman. Miraculously, the woman was healed! She is alive to this day—clear of any cancer! As expected, her husband made Jesus Lord of his life and was baptized!

Sisters, we can read these stories and wonder why God doesn't pull through for us. Remember, prayers are *requests* to God—not orders. Prayer is not about us. It's all about our heavenly Father. Do you get all your wishes from your parents? No. Do you, as a parent, fulfill every desire for your children? No. We always give them a response, but it is not necessarily what our children want. Does that make us mean or bad parents? No, I do not believe so.

My children have been begging me for a dog since they were little. Honestly, I was not ready for a dog for many years. Though I love my children, I didn't believe that we were able to handle another living being in our home without it causing chaos. Finally, as my girls matured into teenagers, I thought that we could manage a dog. So now, we have a cute little Maltese.

Most of you mothers can relate to me. And even if you aren't a mother, you can imagine how it would feel to have little children running around, a household to take care of, a husband to cook for and laundry to do, but on top of that, to have a puppy who needs toilet training, feeding and attention. There is only so much that one family can handle. In the same way, God knows how much we can handle, and he gives us his blessings in the right way and at the right times.

But why do we women give up easily, especially in prayer? I was listening to a radio program about how men are more goal-oriented than women. Women are mood-oriented. Now, this is just a generalization and may not apply to all men and women. But on the whole, a woman would rather receive a diamond necklace or a certificate to the spa than a vacuum cleaner or mixer for Christmas.

Being goal-oriented beings, men look at the practical necessities. They want the house clean or good food to eat, so they will tend to buy handy items as gifts.

Women, being feeling-oriented, would desire jewelry, because it is romantic.

So what does this have to do with prayer? We probably pray the same way—a man would pray for his job to do well and for him to be successful, while a woman would pray to have a happy marriage and a peaceful home.

So when we *feel* like God is not answering our prayers the way we *feel* that he should, we give up because we don't *feel* like praying any more. Does this make sense to some of you? For men, as long as the goal is still there, they will keep on going. The goal is what motivates them not to give up. For women, a goal can become oppressive—a source of stress and insecurity. Somewhere our minds play with our hearts—*What if I don't make it? What if it doesn't work out? What if I was stretching too far, beyond what I can attain?* These mind games make us give up.

Jesus is speaking to you right now. Will he find faith in your heart? Do you hear his message asking you not to stop praying? Remember, Jesus knows what it is like *not* to get a prayer answered *his* way. In fact, his final prayer request was uttered in the Garden of Gethsemane with loud cries and tears as he sweat drops of blood begging for a way other than the cross. He left it to God's will, however. He submitted to God's decision. The prayers were not answered the way Jesus wanted, but he still trusted in his Father. Though he prayed, it did not prevent him from suffering in this world. We are called to keep on praying just like our Lord.

> During the days of Jesus' life on earth, he offered up prayers and petitions with loud cries and tears to the one who could save him from death, and he was heard because of his reverent submission. Although he was a son, he learned obedience from what he suffered. (Hebrews 5:7-8)

Do you hear the thunder? Do you smell the incense? Do you see the hosts of angels carrying the golden bowls? Do you see the fire? Maybe, you don't, but God does. It is the result of all your prayers. It is truly a mystery that none of us will ever fully comprehend. Even as Jesus faced the greatest challenge in his life, God had a different answer to his prayers. This did not change or influence the way that Jesus prayed. He prayed faithfully trusting in his Father even on the cross as he took our sins upon his frail body.

Dear sisters, let us follow our Lord Jesus to the cross as we continue to persevere in prayer. Our heavenly Maker and Creator will strengthen us and protect us from the evil one as we rely on him.

~

STUDY QUESTIONS

Prayer: Why Do It When God Already Knows?

1. Many times we do not understand the ways that God is working through prayer. We often cling to "worthless" things in our lives when God wants to give us so many more blessings. How have you surrendered to God in prayer? Are you relying on God to help you during both the good and dark times in your life?

2. Elijah lived during sinful and dark times. He prayed a lot during the famine when there was no food and water. We need to learn from Elijah and keep praying through hopeless times. What can you learn from Elijah's life as he prayed during the tough times? Do you keep your faith in prayer even when a situation is looking grim?

3. Jesus says that we only need a mustard seed of faith for him to move mountains. Think about your faith and the different prayer requests that you have had recently. Have you been allowing God's responses to influence your faith?

a. Make a decision to pray with others consistently.

b. Try to challenge your faith in prayer and allow that mustard seed of faith to increase as you persevere in your prayer life.

c. Think through the obstacles in your faith and start praying about those hindrances so that you can overcome.

7

God's Church

WHY DO I NEED FAMILY?

For just as we have many members in one body and all the
members do not have the same function, so we, who are
many, are one body in Christ, and individually members
one of another.

Romans 12:4-5 (NASV)

1
GOD IS ALL ABOUT COMMUNITY

"Betsy"[1] stood on the ledge of a high-rise in Tokyo, Japan. She
had been involved in drugs, alcohol and sexual relationships with
men. She had run away from the Philippines to find a "better" life in
Japan but was met with the same emptiness as in her homeland. She
had a cell phone in her pocket which rang as she was ready to
plunge to her death. *Maybe God wants me to answer that phone call.
No, I don't want to. I want to die—nobody is going to stop me.* It kept
ringing. *I wish this phone would just shut up! I'll just drop it from this
height.* Yet, something inside of Betsy made her answer the call.

"Hi Betsy, what are you up to? I miss you. I love you," said the
caller.

Those words were a lightning bolt through her bruised and
pain-filled heart.

"Uh. I'm not fine. I am going to die tonight."

"No, you can't die tonight. You are one of my best friends. I need you."

"You don't need me. Nobody needs me. I am worthless."

"Now, what are you up to? You need to just sit down in your living room and wait for me because I am going to be at your place in just a few minutes. I'll talk to you while I am making my way there."

The caller had received a telephone message from Betsy's husband who was in the Philippines. Earlier that day, he had received a cryptic message from his wife. Basically, she told her estranged husband that she was going to end her misery. The caller was a special friend of Betsy's from church. Betsy's estranged husband, Grant,[2] was a faithful Christian praying for his "prodigal" wife. Even though Betsy had left God to follow her sinful ways, the Christians, including her husband, never stopped trying to reach out to Betsy. They loved her very much.

Life does not work out as we planned. For some of us, it is easy to get on the ledge and believe that there is no hope. God knows that we are weak without the aid of others.

> Two are better than one
>   because they have a good return for their labor.
> For if either of them falls,
>   the one will lift up his companion.
> (Ecclesiastes 4:9-10, NASV)

This scripture describes our need for others—relationships that will get us through when we stumble, when we fall and when we fail. For this reason, God created *family*—a group of people whom we can turn to and receive strength from. This family is not necessarily our physical family, but is rather the church of our Lord Jesus Christ. When we look at the very nature of God, he is all about community and family.

God is not a singular being. In the Scriptures, God describes himself in the plural form. Even as he creates the world, he says, "Let *us* create man in *our* image, in *our* likeness," speaking of his relationship with Jesus and the Holy Spirit (Genesis 1:26, emphasis added). God's likeness is not seen in our physical appearance but rather in terms of our spiritual nature—God's characteristics and his needs. God's very essence is plurality—through it, he defines love. He loves community. He values family. When he created man, he saw that it was "not good for the man to be alone" (Genesis 2:18). He, therefore, made woman to be with man. He then commanded them to be fruitful and to multiply—once again, encouraging community and family.

Relationships are what teach us the very definition of love—the very core of God. All alone, none of us can truly understand love. In fact, the Bible teaches that God is love. God's love is made complete in us when we love one another (1 John 4:12). Without the fellowship of believers, it is hard to understand God's love. Sometimes, we find it hard to see and to feel God's love. We can experience loneliness at work or even at home on any given day. We can be isolated on a university campus as we go from class to class. We can even be at church and feel completely separate from everyone else. God wants us to be connected.

It was the love of family—a spiritual sister—that kept Betsy from jumping off the ledge. The caller kept talking to her as she approached her building, coaxed her to go inside her apartment, convinced her to get off the window ledge and made her sit on her sofa where she began to weep as she opened her heart to the caller. The woman was a close friend—a friend that Betsy had forgotten she had, in the midst of her distress, and a sister in the Lord who really cared about her. The caller brought another friend from church with her to be a support for Betsy through her rough time. Betsy felt their love and saw God's love through these two special people. It was a turning point in her life as she decided to rededicate her life to God and return to her home in the Philippines where her husband waited for her with open arms.

Grant still loved Betsy despite what she had done with her life. He could not judge or accuse her because in the past he, too, had sinned against God, leaving his faith to live a worldly life for many years. He had only recently recommitted his life to Christ and knew that he needed to love his wife through her mistakes so that she, too, could change and return to God.

God used a community of believers to save Grant and Betsy's souls. They are happily married to this day. Both of them saw the emptiness of the world but needed the helping hand of friends in Christ. When they could not see or feel God's love, the brothers and sisters in the church reached out with their hearts and poured out what God had given them. These loving Christians went out on a limb, and now Grant and Betsy are grateful for the church and their relationships there. It was through God's community that they have remained faithful to this day, overcoming the scars of their past.

In the same way, every Christian needs the aid of other brothers and sisters. We need others in our lives who are willing to encourage and support our faith. It is during the worst times that we often need the encouragement of others. Yet, it is at those times that we can often distance ourselves from our friendships in the church, preventing us from getting our needs met.

> Take care, brethren, that there not be in any one of you an evil, unbelieving heart that falls away from the living God. But encourage one another day after day, as long as it is still called "Today," so that none of you will be hardened by the deceitfulness of sin. (Hebrews 3:12-13, NASV)

Encouragement should be a daily habit, not just when someone seems down. Unbelief, doubts and sin are a constant threat for the Christian who tries her best for God. The daily words of affirmation and love help keep our belief in God strong—without it, it is nearly impossible. God knows this about each one of us. That is why he created the church—the body of believers and community of followers—to be his family and children.

The true evidence of our commitment to Jesus is our love for one another (1 John 4:7–12). This love is to be the same as that of Jesus Christ, who gave his life for us. Without this level of love, we cannot be held together. Yet, at the same time, no one in the church is perfect. It is made up of defective and faulty human beings. Because of this, God's community can have its failings and hurtful sides as well.

The good news is that all these deficient and imperfect individuals can make up for one another's shortcomings. The collective members make up a perfect family, as long as there is grace for one another. Grace is the key to making the church God's true community.

> A new commandment I give to you, that you love one another, even as I have loved you, that you also love one another. By this all men will know that you are My disciples, if you have love for one another. (John 13:34–35, NASV)

2

THE CHURCH IS A SPIRITUAL KINGDOM

The kingdom of God. The kingdom of heaven. The heavenly realms. You have heard these words and phrases over and over again—through the sermons of our favorite preachers as well as in Jesus' teachings. These phrases are found throughout the New Testament, especially in the Gospels. In the Gospel of Matthew, the writer refers to the "kingdom of heaven" thirty-three times, with the concept being mentioned fifty times. Most of the time that Matthew mentions the kingdom, he uses "heaven" instead of "God." His use of Jewish phraseology "kingdom of heaven" and "Father in heaven" reveals the Jewish reverential reluctance to use the name "God."[3] Consequently, the expression "kingdom of God" is used only four times in the book of Matthew.

In the Gospel of Mark, the writer uses the phrase, "kingdom of God" thirteen times, but refers to the kingdom about twenty times throughout the Gospel. Similarly, the Gospel of Luke also uses the expression "kingdom of God," referring to this theme over forty times in his Gospel.

Finally, unlike the other Gospels, the book of John mentions the kingdom only in chapters 3 and 18. Yet, John explains in the third chapter how to enter the kingdom of God. Regardless of the number of times, it is clear that "the kingdom" is one of the central themes in Jesus' preaching.

When we hear the word "kingdom," it conjures up an image of a place where there is a king, queen and a castle of some kind. Even the disciples thought that Jesus was talking about an earthly kingdom when he preached about its appearing. James and John wanted to be seated at Jesus' right and left when the kingdom came (Mark 10:37). Yet, an earthly kingdom was not what God had in mind.

If in his spiritual kingdom God is the king with Jesus alongside him, then we, as Christians, are his royal subjects and his imperial children who serve in this realm. In fact, the Bible tells us that we are a "royal priesthood."

> But you are a chosen race, a royal priesthood, a holy nation, a people for God's own possession, so that you may proclaim the excellencies of Him who has called you out of darkness into His marvelous light.
> (1 Peter 2:9, NASV)

The simple gathering of believers that we see each Sunday is a group of royalty! They are part of a holy nation, belonging to God.

We are a part of God's royal family, held together in his realm of light. More than that, we are princes and princesses in God's regal nation, bonded by the blood of Jesus Christ. His blood runs through our soul and spirit, cleansing us of sins, daily. What an incredible privilege to be called by him and to be chosen to partake in this exceptional family and kingdom! Consequently our real citizenship is in heaven, not in the particular nation/state where we live (Philippians 3:20), and there is where our ultimate loyalty lies.

While I was living in Japan, my widowed father remarried. He had a grand wedding attended by many dignitaries including Japan's royal family. It was an honor to have such important individuals present at my father's wedding. The royal family in Japan does not normally attend weddings of "commoners," yet they took the time to celebrate with my father and his new wife. Our family felt very special because of their presence.

In the same way, it is a privilege and honor to share time with God's royal family—the brothers and sisters in the church. Each member of the church is part of the royal priesthood.

They are not only royal but holy. When we learn to look at one another, not just as "Nick," "Marianne," "Tom" or "Joyce," but as true princes and princesses in God's imperial realm, we will begin to cherish, respect and honor one another. Going to church will become a special event, not another obligation in our schedules. Even gathering with fellow disciples during the week will seem like a privilege.

A couple of years after my father's wedding, my husband and I were able to attend a special reception with the Prince and Princess of Japan. We conversed with both of them for a long time. It was a dream come true to be able to share about our mission work in Japan with them. They were extremely kind and gracious to us. Yet, during our conversation, we were not allowed to touch them or get too close to them. There were secret service men everywhere, guarding them and protecting them. The security was intense.

Scripture teaches that God protects his royal family in much the same manner. He has his angels guarding us from the onslaughts of Satan. God's secret service is invisible but very real. They reside in the spiritual realm, keeping watch over our souls as we do battle in this world. Our King, who is our heavenly Father, cherishes our faith and soul. Even though we might not "feel" the unseen presence of his guards, they are there beside us each day. In this crooked and depraved world, God sees us as lights flickering in the darkness (Philippians 2:15). He does not want those lights to go out. Every one of them is precious in his sight.

As lights in the darkness, when we come together to worship our King, our collective sparks ignite to become a flame. This flame empowers us to face the workplace, school, neighborhood and even foreign countries with confidence and faith. This fire will increase our faith and encourage us to remain faithful. We need one another. We need the fellowship. We need the relationships which help us to get open and real.[4]

As we grow to recognize God's kingdom as a place of honor, let us also learn to appreciate the special relationships that we have in the church. We have been chosen to be members of a remarkable kingdom—the heavenly realm. What could be better than being the child of the King of kings and the Lord of lords? Understand that you are precious and holy to him. Though we do not deserve such treatment, God has seated you in his heavenly realm to be with him now and forevermore.

> And God raised us up with Christ and seated us with him in the heavenly realms in Christ Jesus, in order that in the coming ages he might show the incomparable riches of his grace, expressed in his kindness to us in Christ Jesus. (Ephesians 2:6-7)

3

Jesus' Sacrifice for the Church

In a remote rural village of China, a young woman became pregnant with a child. All the family rejoiced with the tidings of the new arrival. Shortly thereafter, however, the good news was met with great distress as the doctor informed the young couple that the mother would die if she gave birth to the child. He advised them to end the pregnancy before it was too late.

This young woman was grief-stricken with the choice between killing her own child to save her own life and dying in order to preserve the life of her unborn child. With much tears and pain, the mother decided to keep her child and die. It was more important for her to give life than to take it away. She was consoled by the fact that her husband could raise the child for her.

Just as the doctor predicted, the mother died during childbirth, bringing a healthy baby boy into the world with her last breath. The father was overwhelmed with grief as he had hoped against all hope that his wife would somehow survive the delivery.

After his wife's death, the grieving father was faced with another important decision. He was not confident about raising the child on his own, so he took the baby across the river to a village where his good friend lived. He asked his friend and his wife to take care of the baby for him as he felt that he would be inadequate for the task. He asked them to raise the boy as their own son.

The father's friend took the baby. With many tears, the father left the village resolute never to see his son again, at least until he was fully grown. The baby, "Tony,"[5] grew up into a very handsome and smart young man. When the time was right, his adoptive parents told him the story about his real father who brought him across the river when he was just a newborn. This infuriated the young man as he could not understand why his real parent would give him up. His adoptive father told Tony that they could visit his real father across the river and inquire why he had made that choice.

When they arrived at Tony's biological father's home, he recognized Tony right away; he was an exact image of his wife's father. He was also with his friend from across the river, and he was the age he calculated him to be, as he had remembered his birthday every year.

"Hello, my name is Tony. My father told me that you are my real father. I am here to understand why you made the decision to abandon me as a baby."

The biological father was overcome with emotion and held back his tears at the sight of his son.

"Come and sit down. I will make some tea and explain everything to you."

His real father began, "Tony, when your mother became pregnant with you, we were told that we should give up the baby so that she could live. She had a kidney problem that would cause her to die if she gave birth to you. Your mother made a very difficult decision that only she could make. She wanted you to have life. Even at her young age, she was not willing to sacrifice your life so that she could live. We hoped that somehow she would survive the birth despite what the doctors said. Tony, she died during childbirth, but you are alive!" At this, his real father's eyes welled up in tears.

"I miss your mother. She was a good woman," he told him.

Tony was stunned to hear the actual story. His eyes filled with tears as he had never felt such love before in his life. Someone that he had never met in his whole life had actually died for him, so that he could live. His parents did not hate him or despise him but rather loved him beyond his imagination. He was amazed by the love of his biological father and mother. It was more important to them that Tony have a chance at life, even though it meant that they would both have to suffer. His biological father missed his wife dearly and had lost his son at the same time.

After a moment of silence and emotion, his biological father continued, "You see, Tony, I was a young man who didn't feel adequate to raise a child alone—without the help of your mother. It was a hard choice for me to give you up after losing my wife. As much as I wanted to keep you, I knew that I couldn't do a good job raising you. That's why I brought you across the river to my friend's house, who I believed, would love you and raise you properly. As much as I wanted to keep you, I knew I couldn't do it."

With this explanation, Tony's life was transformed. He left with a deep understanding that he was not an "unwanted" child but rather one that was loved deeply—far beyond what he could have ever imagined. He had a great appreciation for his biological father and mother, and at the same time, he was also thankful for the two people who adopted him and raised him as their own son. His life had more significance knowing these truths.

After learning about the sacrifice of his parents to enable him to live, he reasoned that he was meant to do something special with his life.

Just a couple of years later, while at university, Tony met some missionaries. They began to open the Scriptures to him about the sacrifice of Jesus. His heart ached as he understood the cross. The missionaries were amazed how quickly Tony comprehended Christ's sacrifice. For most of the Chinese, it took longer and more explanation to grasp the concept of an unknown man dying many centuries ago to give them eternal life.

When they asked him why he was so moved by the cross, Tony explained the story of his mother to the missionaries. Her sacrifice many years ago now had even deeper meaning. She not only gave Tony life, but a chance for eternal life in Christ as a result of her sacrifice. Presently, Tony is a minister for an underground church in China. His life has been an example of sacrifice and love as hundreds gather together to worship Jesus.

Tony's story of total love and surrender touches the hearts of many. The Bible tells the same story about God's sacrifice. Yet, his offering was not for one man but for all of mankind. It was the ultimate sacrifice of love. Through God's supreme offering, Christ was able to establish his church—his family.

> In bringing many sons to glory, it was fitting that God, for whom and through whom everything exists, should make the author of their salvation perfect through suffering. Both the one who makes men holy and those who are made holy are of the same family. So Jesus is not ashamed to call them brothers. (Hebrews 2:10-11)

> ...just as Christ loved the church and gave himself up for her to make her holy, cleansing her by the washing with water through the word, and to present her to himself as a radiant church, without stain or wrinkle or any other blemish, but holy and blameless. (Ephesians 5:25-27)

We are made holy through Christ's sacrifice. It is what allows us to be a part of his family. His blood made us blameless and clean. The cost for being "family" with God—a part of Christ's church—is Jesus' sacrifice. Without his suffering on the cross, we would still be drowning in our sins and devoid of hope. Christ won the battle against death and the powers of evil when he rose from the dead. He was the firstborn from among the dead making him the head of the body, the church (Colossians 1:18).

This kind of sacrifice is unique. It is hard for any human being to call themselves to the same standard as Jesus. Many Christians do not connect this concept in their personal lives—that God expects us to sacrifice for our brothers and sisters in the church in the same manner. God has freely given us his grace. If we have gratitude and love in our hearts, we will grant the same form of mercy and grace to those in the body of believers. And when we go the "extra mile" through loving first, we can be like Christ in our relationship with others.

Tony's mother's sacrifice was not wasted on Tony. In fact, it was the key to showing Tony the significance of Christ's love. Moreover, Christ's mercy and forgiveness was not left without effect in his life either. Tony's whole life is devoted to saving the souls of his people and to keeping them faithful to God. Let us be encouraged by this brother in China and do the same by dedicating our lives to sacrifice—for the church, our family of believers.

We will not all become leaders in the church, but we certainly can offer our best to the brothers and sisters around us as Christ has done for us. This may be accomplished through our efforts to serve, to clean, to encourage or to share. We have a wonderful opportunity through the family of believers to be a light to the world. If each one of us makes the effort, the church will truly become an amazing family.

> Let us not become weary in doing good, for at the proper time we will reap a harvest if we do not give up. Therefore, as we have opportunity, let us do good to all people, especially to those who belong to the family of believers. (Galatians 6:9-10)

4

ACTIVELY SERVING IN GOD'S COMMUNITY

What does it mean for a Christian to be a part of God's community? What is the importance of our roles? How can we serve in the church and be used to help the body of believers? To God, each one of us is a vital part of the body of Christ. We each add a special quality and flavor to the fellowship that no one else can. God allows for us to use our unique talents, gifts and even disabilities to build up the body of Christ.

> There are different kinds of gifts, but the same Spirit. There are different kinds of service, but the same Lord. There are different kinds of working, but the same God works all of them in all men. (1 Corinthians 12:4-6)

God gives each one of us his Spirit. Yet, the same Spirit manifests in every Christian differently. This does not make one person more important or more crucial to the body than another. God tells us that even the weakest member of the fellowship is indispensable (1 Corinthians 12:21–22). Each of us has a special gift from God that is unique to us. This means every Christian adds something very needed to God's church, making it a vibrant family—built together by God's Holy Spirit—not a man-made organization.

As women, we wonder how we can help or serve in the church. We may look at ourselves and fail to see our distinctive abilities and strengths. As a result, we wait for others to give us an assignment before taking the initiative. When no one approaches us with a specific task, we assume that we are useless. God does not want us to waste away in the fellowship like this.

At the same time, it can be tempting for us to desire to be in a position of importance, so instead of volunteering to help clean the church building, we wait for someone to give us a more significant task like teaching a class or running a women's program. The more important that we feel in the fellowship, the closer we can feel to God.

As Christians, when we get caught up in the temptations of selfish ambition or, on the other extreme, devaluing our importance, we need to remember Christ's attitude. No one can grow closer to God through her role or worth in the church. In fact, each one of us is equally essential in God's kingdom.

> Your attitude should be the same as that Christ Jesus:
> Who, being in very nature God, did not consider equal-
> ity with God something to be grasped, but made himself
> nothing, taking the very nature of a servant. (Philippians
> 2:5-7a)

Jesus did not come into the world to be served but to serve. In fact, the word translated "servant" is a word that actually means "slave." So, Jesus came to take on the very nature of a slave. More than that, he came into this world to be a ransom for all of mankind (Mark 10:45). Similarly, if we want to be regarded as "great" in his kingdom, we must begin with the attitude of a servant (Matthew 20:26). Accordingly, those who want to become first or "greatest" must be slave to those around them (Matthew 20:27). We can understand this concept in our heads easier than in our hearts. Somewhere in each of us, we desire respect, honor and admiration. Our goal and aspiration in life is not to become a *slave*.

According to American history, slaves were the most ill-treated people from the time of the early settlers. Slaves were crammed into boats with no sunlight for months and brought to the Americas. Once they arrived at the ports, they were chained and sold to the highest bidders. If they did not obey their masters, they were whipped and beaten. Some of these slaves were even beaten to death. Their masters had the right to do anything they pleased to these unprotected individuals.

In the excerpt below, a little five-year-old boy was abused and beaten as a slave:

> The boy had been so abused and badly beaten in
> slavery in Alabama that, afraid to displease his master, he
> denied having a mother in that area. When she saw him,
> Peter refused to acknowledge her, and claimed that his
> scars had been caused by accidents. The terrified boy

pleaded not to be taken from his master, but the judge ruled that he should be returned to his mother. When she was finally able to quiet his fears, Isabella found that her child's body was covered with sores and scars. Fowler had beaten him, he said.

When she asked how Fowler's wife, Eliza, her master's sister, had reacted when he was abused in this way, he replied: "Sometimes I crawled under the stoop, mammy, the blood running all about me, and my back would stick to the boards; and sometimes Miss Eliza would come and grease my sores, when all were abed and asleep."

The painful memories of slavery, of temporarily losing her son, and of Pete's brutal treatment in the South fueled the power and passion of Isabella's later work as an antislavery speaker and women's rights advocate. By then she had changed her name to Sojourner Truth.[6]

Imagine being a slave in the United States—having your children sold, being whipped, being separated from your family to be sold. Slavery in Jesus' time may have been even more harsh and cruel. The most amazing detail about this teaching is that Jesus did not teach anything that he himself did not undergo or do. Whatever the slaves of his time faced, he allowed himself to experience in order to show his love and grace. Jesus was falsely accused of wrongdoing, whipped, beaten and abused when he had done nothing wrong. When Jesus hung on the cross, he was separated from his Father in heaven as he took the sins of man upon himself (2 Corinthians 5:21, Isaiah 59:1–2). He was brutally tortured and murdered.

For many churchgoers in America, church has become a place where "I get encouraged"; where "I need to be served"; where "I need to hear a good sermon or else I'm not coming back." It is sad that Jesus' teachings for each Christian to serve and to encourage have gotten lost in many of our fellowships. It is actually a privilege to serve in God's kingdom—and it does not matter how or in what role. No matter who we are or who we are not, we can add to the body of believers in an incredible way.

> For we are God's workmanship, created in Christ Jesus to do good works, which God prepared in advance for us to do. (Ephesians 2:10)

5

ALLOWING FRIENDSHIPS TO KEEP YOU FAITHFUL

> I pray that you, being rooted and established in love, may have power, together with all the saints, to grasp how wide and long and high and deep is the love of Christ, and to know this love that surpasses knowledge—that you may be filled to the measure of all the fullness of God. (Ephesians 3:17b-19)

Paul prays for the Ephesians that they may have power, together with all the saints, to grasp the magnificent love of Christ—its width, its length, its height and its depth. Without others, we cannot grasp this love that surpasses knowledge. It will fill us with the measure of all the fullness of God if we allow it to. Satan wants us to mistrust the church. If he can convince us that God's church is a man-made organization that has nothing to do with God, then he has convinced us to never fully experience the love of Christ.

In fact, we need the fellowship of God's people to survive spiritually. When God's people gather together, there is a spiritual power that begins to work. This power is invisible to the naked eye.

> "For where two or three *come together* in my name, there am I with them." (Matthew 18:20, emphasis added)

Just imagine the Holy Spirit of God inside each of us as we gather to fellowship and hear God's word. He burns within us as we hear spiritual preaching! Moreover, we become united in worship to God through God's Spirit.

This bond is also evident in the Old Testament as two spiritual men, Jonathan and David, shared deep fellowship because of their love for one another. Their love united them to become one in spirit (1 Samuel 18:1).

This special friendship between Jonathan and David was not just based on "clicking" or getting along because of personality or shared hobbies. There was a mutual respect, love and loyalty based on their relationship with God. It went far beyond age, title, role or background. In fact, Jonathan made a covenant with David, giving him his robe, tunic, sword, bow and belt. He loved David as himself (1 Samuel 18:3–4). Jonathan, the prince of Israel, gave his most treasured possessions, all of which represented his monarchy and status, to a mere shepherd boy! Jonathan could have just given him his sword or bow, but, instead, he gave David his tunic, robe and belt as well.

Jonathan was left looking like a pauper after giving away his weapons and clothes! He did it not only for his friendship with David, but he was affirming the will of God by showing his acceptance of David as the heir to the throne. The interesting fact is that David gave Jonathan nothing in return for these precious gifts. David accepted them, and they were bonded in spirit.

As women, we are connecters and bonders. We need friendships that get us through the tough times in life. Those friendships do not come easily, however. They come at a price. Loyalty and love are earned by the loyalty and love that we give to others. We may want these kinds of relationships but have put walls around ourselves to avoid hurts. Granted, many of us may have been hurt by relationships in our church—especially by people to whom we gave our complete trust and love. But there are other women out there who yearn and desire a relationship with you—the same kind that you so desperately need.

When women come together, they cry; they comfort; they touch, and they encourage. Women know how to console and reassure one another like no man can. That is why women need other women in their lives to help them feel secure and loved. They also know how to express love and encouragement with just the right words to heal, to bond and to sympathize.

Because of this, many women are great authors of romantic novels with their ability to articulate deep, passionate and meaningful words. Some of the most romantic writings are not written by men but by women! Women like Charlotte Bronte who wrote *Jane Eyre;* Jane Austen who wrote *Pride and Prejudice;* Emily Bronte who wrote *Wuthering Heights;* Margaret Mitchell who wrote *Gone with the Wind;* Emily Dickinson with her poems filled with passion and intensity. And the Bible even includes Ruth's vows to her mother-in-law, Naomi—till death do us part—and we use that scripture in weddings!

When we women get together, we don't try to fix each other. We listen to one another, and it doesn't matter how many details there are to that one meal or to that one event—every detail is intriguing and important to listen to. We share about our horrible pap smears, our health problems, our children, our fears, and we understand one another because as women we view things similarly. When God gives us friendships, it is a gift. It is an answer to prayer. It is a blessing never to be taken for granted.

True friendships need to be fought for, sacrificed for and given tons of grace. No real friendship is without its difficulties, hurts and misunderstandings. To believe that a perfect relationship has no hurts is unrealistic and unfair for the other person. There is always a time when one friend will need the other more or when one is more dependent on the other.

Of course, we need to remember that God is the only one who can truly fill the void of loneliness and give us true happiness. We cannot expect our friends to give us all the happiness and fulfillment that we want. Even Jesus experienced the deepest hurt from his closest relationships when his disciples betrayed and abandoned him. He restored his relationships by taking the initiative to sacrifice.

As much as we women are good at bonding, we can also cause emotional drama in our friendships. For all the times we remember people's birthdays, anniversaries and special days, we also can dwell on hurts and say needless, hurtful words out of our emotional outbursts.

This is why we need Jesus to be at the center of our friendships. When we understand true fellowship and real spiritual relationships in the Lord's kingdom, the eyes of our heart will be opened to see Jesus more clearly. These relationships will not only help us stay close to God but will also help us to understand Christ's love. These friendships are essential. Sometimes we will not be able to find the strength within ourselves, so we need spiritual girlfriends to get us through. Getting another perspective helps us to see the situation in a more objective way.

What, then, is the kingdom of God and the kingdom of heaven? It is God's way of helping us to stay connected to Jesus and to God spiritually. It is God's home and family. It is a spiritual haven for our souls. It is a link to our salvation and is essential for us to stay faithful to the Lord. It is being part of a colony of heaven on this earth. God paid a high price to establish his kingdom, his reign in our lives. It comes at the sacrifice of his one and only Son (Ephesians 5:25–27). When we are rooted and established in love with true heartfelt relationships, we can, with the help of other Christian women, gain an understanding of Christ's love and be filled with all the fullness of God.

In the Gospel of Matthew, Jesus describes how the kingdom of heaven is like a treasure hidden in the field. When someone finds it, he will sell all he has to buy that field (Matthew 13:44). When we understand the true worth of the kingdom of God, we will be willing to sacrifice a great deal for it. It is an incredible treasure in God's sight. The message of Jesus focused on the centrality of the kingdom of God in the Gospels.

We need to realize what incredible blessings we have through God's church and also know that it is within reach for each of us to see and to understand God and his kingdom better. God wants us to open the eyes of our hearts in the heavenly realms. In doing so, we will have deeper and more lasting relationships which will, in turn, teach us increasingly more about God's grace and love.

∽

STUDY QUESTIONS

God's Church: Why Do I Need Family?

1. Think about the church you attend right now. Who are the people that you encourage daily? Who are the people who help you? Have you distanced yourself from the fellowship lately? What will you do to reconnect yourself?

   a. There are definitely people in your church who need extra help. They may be going through a divorce, hurting over a loss or death, or some other situation. Think about how you can show them "family" by your love and encouragement at this time.

   b. If you do not feel adequate to help someone who is hurting or in need, just tell them that you will be praying for them as they go through their challenges…and then remember to actually do it!

2. God's kingdom is a realm of royalty: the children of God. All of us are a part of God's royal priesthood—made holy and blameless

in his sight. How can you change your view of the people at church who are more difficult ones for you to love? How will this help your relationships within your fellowship?

3. Jesus made some incredible sacrifices for the church. He was not only a servant, but a slave to all of mankind. How can we imitate his heart to serve others? Who are the people in your life who need your sacrifice and support?

4. Do you have relationships that keep you encouraged in your faith? Have you been a "Jonathan" to someone in your fellowship?

   a. Who are you bonded with in the Spirit?

   b. How have you sacrificed or not sacrificed for that relationship?

   c. How can you grow in your friendships in the church?

Hell

Is There Really a Place of Condemnation?

Honestly, this was the most challenging chapter for me to write. I struggled over the content and went through many rewrites. I asked close friends as well as my husband to help me through the different beliefs about hell—whether from Scriptures or from famous writers. No matter who you are, hell is a scary concept. Hopefully, the ideas and views presented in this chapter will be enlightening for you. Remember, none of us has been there and, Lord willing, none of you who are reading this chapter will ever go there. But we need to be aware of its existence.

As women, give us the warm fuzzies, and we're *there*. We like to hear about heaven and angels, but when it comes to hell, we would rather skip the subject. In fact, the topic sounds creepy and frightening. Satan is enough to deal with, but hell? We would rather get a manicure or catch a chick flick. Some might have even been tempted to skip this chapter all together.

While living in Japan, I studied the Bible with an elderly woman named Toshiko who had been through a near-death experience. At the age of forty-five, she had suffered a stroke that put her in the hospital for weeks. She was unconscious and had no heartbeat when she first arrived into the emergency room. Throughout that time of unconsciousness, she had a "dream" that was terrifying. It was the worst nightmare that she had ever had.

Toshiko felt her body floating away toward a light. As she approached the light, she saw her long-deceased mother. She felt so much joy that her eyes welled up with tears, and she tried to draw closer to her mother. Just a moment before she reached her mother, the image of her mother transformed into a frightening beast.

Fear filled her heart at the sight of the demon. Toshiko recoiled and tried to run away. Meanwhile, the creature laughed and tried to grab her while taunting her for crying out to her mother. Just as the creature was about to seize Toshiko, she awoke to find herself on the emergency room table. Her heartbeat had started again. She was successfully revived.

As Toshiko told me the story of her horrible nightmare, it brought chills down my spine. There was genuine fear in her eyes when she recounted her experience with death. Her heart had stopped for just five minutes. She was confused and disturbed by this dream for years. She could not understand why her mother would turn into a demon. She could not comprehend why God would send her to hell. I cannot say whether what she saw was real or not. But her dream was real to her.

For most Christians, there is a genuine fear of hell, and so many of us avoid the subject. Because hell can be such an unpleasant topic, more and more people in the Christian world even deny its existence:

> For Long [a man's name], hell is all too real—a temporary torment in this life, an endless agony in the next. But for more and more Americans, hell is a myth.
>
> In a survey released this summer by the Pew Forum on Religion & Public Life, just 59 percent of 35,000 respondents said they believe in a hell "where people who have led bad lives, and die without being sorry, are eternally punished."

That's down from the 71 percent who said they believed in hell in a 2001 Gallup survey. And it is lower than the 74 percent who said they believe in heaven in the recent Pew poll.

…"They believe everyone has an equal chance, at this life and the next," said Alan Segal, a professor of religion at Barnard College and the author of "Life After Death: A History of the Afterlife in Western Religion."

"So hell is disappearing, absolutely."

But for those who believe, hell can be a terrifying place of eternal punishment or the complete extinction of the soul.[1]

In this age of political correctness, fewer and fewer preachers talk about hell seriously. It has become more of a story or fairy tale. As much as we would want to rationalize or to deny the existence of eternal damnation, Jesus makes it clear that there is a place where many will pay the penalty eternally. Moreover, the Apostle John wrote in the book of Revelation that "hell" is eternal torment—the place where the devil and the false prophet are going to be sent—their punishment lasting day and night forever and ever (Revelation 20:10).

Many of us can accept that the devil and his false prophets will be condemned to eternal condemnation. However, imagining "dear old Aunt Mae" or "our sweet non-believing neighbor across the street" going to hell can seem difficult and even inconceivable. It is easy for us to get hazy in our convictions about where the lines of God's justice and mercy are drawn. It is easier to rationalize and make excuses for people when they are "nice" or "good" people.

What has put such fear in us to keep us from exploring and understanding hell more in-depth? Why do we avoid a subject that Jesus was not afraid to preach about? When we look at history, during the Middle Ages, a famous writer by the name of Dante Alighieri (1265–1321) profoundly altered the common Christian view of hell and demons by the graphic imagery he employed in his writings known as *Dante's Inferno*. He depicted a place of punishment with many levels of torture and pain. The suffering is inflicted by demons with Satan as the head of all cruelty. In the following passage the devil is depicted as having three faces, and as feeding on sinners in his grasp:

> At every mouth he with his teeth was crunching
> A sinner, in the manner of a brake,
> ...and down three chins
> Trickled the tear-drops and the bloody drivel.
> Dante's Inferno Canto 34.55 [2]

Sadly, during the Dark Ages, church priests used these writings for the set purpose of instilling fear in the average parishioner. Historically, the church went apostate in many areas of Europe at that time. In order to make a living, priests began preaching "fire and brimstone" with forgiveness granted in exchange for gold coins. Accordingly, those priests were the only ones who could take away the people's sins to prevent them from entering into the horrid place of eternal condemnation (1 Timothy 4:1–3).

The concept of forgiveness was taught as having a price tag. Free redemption no longer existed, and people lived in "holy fear." Such false notions have continued through succeeding generations even to the twenty-first century. Unfortunately, for some of us, they have even taken root in our minds. This message of guilt has given many of us misconceptions of God's grace, causing us to live in fear of the fires of hell. We work hard every day trying to be "good" people, but nothing seems to appease the guilt in our hearts despite the fact that we are saved:

> *"I'll just give more money to the poor; then God will be pleased."*
> *"What if I volunteer at church this Sunday—will God be happier with me?"*

"Would God love me more if I was helping more people around me?"
"If I go to church every Sunday, will I receive God's grace and get
into heaven?"

Our own insecurities and anxieties begin to distort our understanding of how God views us. We allow stories, classic literature, media as well as our own accused consciences to influence our thinking more than the Bible. From childhood, these perceptions have become the foundation for our imagination, very little of it based on the word of God. Because of this, we deprive ourselves of understanding God's greatest gift of love: his unconditional grace. These kinds of misconceptions have caused many "good hearted" Christians to be disillusioned with God and to leave their faith. For those people, it is too painful to live with this kind of constant fear and guilt.

The Bible must become our standard. We must not allow ourselves to be influenced more by fictitious stories and films that make us depart from God's truth and blind our hearts to God's message.

1
WHAT IS HELL?

> Then death and the grave were thrown into the lake of fire. This lake of fire is the second death. And anyone whose name was not found recorded in the Book of Life was thrown into the lake of fire.
>
> Revelation 20:14-15 (NLT)

A lake of fire? Is hell a place of burning hot fire and brimstone? Do the condemned burn there forever? Or is it the location where Satan and his demons have their lair, coming up at just the right time to deceive us? Or is it a place of total darkness and separation from God? These are some of the questions Christians often ask.

In the Old Testament the Hebrew word *Sheol* is sometimes used in place of the word "hell." It is translated as "the grave" and sometimes as "the pit." Generally it means the "abode of the dead," both righteous and unrighteous. Perhaps a better understanding is that it is more like Hades, the waiting place of the dead before the final judgment.[3]

The word that is translated "hell" in Jesus' teaching is the word *gehenna,* which means "the valley of Hinnom," a sort of garbage dump outside the city of Jerusalem, communicating that hell is the ending place of wasted lives.

In the New Testament, the Greek words *Hades* (which many see as more of a waiting place) and *Tartarus* are used to refer to places people go after death, but we must be careful in these texts as they don't always refer to the place of punishment Jesus refers to when using the word *gehenna.*

Only Luke's Gospel goes into detail about hell as a place of punishment; although in Matthew it is referred to as a place of "weeping and gnashing of teeth." Whichever words are used in the Bible for hell or the place of punishment, it is a place where the wicked are sent after judgment.

Conversely, it is interesting that heaven is referred to as a place where "he [God] will wipe every tear from [our] eyes. There will be no more death or mourning or crying or pain" (Revelation 21:4). In effect, heaven has neither weeping nor any pain—the exact opposite of hell. Are they, however, truly opposite in every sense? Do the wicked experience eternal (on-going, never-ending) punishment and the righteous eternal bliss?

The fact remains that none of us will completely know what the afterlife is truly like until we see it for ourselves. We can only use our imagination based on Scripture until God calls us to go home to be with him. Even then, God might not allow us to see hell, not even for a moment, because there will be no tears or mourning in heaven.

The Bible, however, does offer us glimpses of the nature of hell. There is much debate about these passages, much of which centers around whether they are to be taken literally or more as parable-like lessons from Jesus. Bible scholars differ in their ideas and perspectives about the very same passages. As a result, I would like to present the two most prevalent perspectives in the conservative Christian world. It may open your eyes to see some of the diverse viewpoints. It is up to you to decide what your view is.

2

The Two Prevalent Views of Hell

When my husband and I went to France and Italy, we visited many cathedrals, churches and chapels. In each of these countries, there were famous artworks—statues, stained glass, paintings or carvings in stone. The frescoes in Italy were breath-taking. The stained glass windows in France were awe-inspiring. All the images were made with extreme precision and incredible details. Through the centuries, the array of colors have faded somewhat, but are still stunning and spectacular to the eye. Interestingly, most of these scenes were about heaven, hell and the judgment. The depictions of hell were especially frightening.

My husband and I could just imagine a peasant or farmer who came to church once every few months from the countryside, because of the distance, to see the church and hear the sermon. As these farmers and their families attended the service, they probably could not help but notice the magnificent images around them—the frescoes, paintings and stained glass windows. They told a story—without words and music. They are a sermon within themselves. In fact, for both my husband and me, the pictures of hell were very scary because they were so vivid. During an age with no TV or video, anyone looking at those images every time they came to church would certainly have a strong picture of hell imprinted on their minds and hearts.

In the same way, most of us have a strong image fixed in our minds about hell. The most well-known image is one of fire, demons and painful suffering for all of eternity. This is the traditional view of hell. Many of us are familiar with the traditional belief that hell lasts forever with the wicked or sinful being tormented for all of eternity, along with Satan and his demons. Traditional thinking interprets scriptures referring to eternal suffering or agony as literal descriptions, citing passages such as Matthew 25:46, where the Bible says that the wicked will go away into "eternal punishment" but the righteous to eternal life. To them eternal torment and eternal suffering are what they say they are, with no other explanation.

Another view of hell is that our souls are doomed to be destroyed in the lake of fire, the second death. Those believing in the destruction of the body and soul, assert that the existence of an unforgiven sinful individual is annihilated after an allotted time of punishment in which they realize they have been cut off from God and from having eternal life. This time of realization and punishment in whatever form is the time of "weeping and gnashing of teeth." Certainly both are "eternal" in their consequences—eternal punishment and eternal nonexistence (after the grief of judgment and separation from God).

"Traditionalists" see in some of Jesus' parables descriptions of hell as a place of eternal suffering. For instance, in the book of Luke, we see the story of the rich man and Lazarus, arguably a parable. Those who lived in greed or without acknowledging the Lord are sent into torment. According to this passage, the rich man is obviously in a place where there is fire and agony.

> "The time came when the beggar died and the angels carried him to Abraham's side. The rich man also died and

was buried. In hell [Hades], where he was in torment, he looked up and saw Abraham far away, with Lazarus by his side. So he called to him, 'Father Abraham, have pity on me and send Lazarus to dip the tip of his finger in water and cool my tongue, because I am in agony in this fire.'"
(Luke 16:22-24)

This famous parable provides an intense depiction of Hades and Paradise. Sometimes the word *Hades* is translated as hell in different versions of the Bible. However, it is quite likely that Hades refers to a waiting place for those who will be judged and consigned to hell when Jesus returns and judges the living and the dead. And in juxtaposition, Paradise (Abraham's bosom) is the waiting place for those who will be welcomed into heaven when Jesus returns. Understanding this possible interpretation of the parable, we will continue.

Lazarus is a beggar who has gone to Paradise alongside Abraham while the rich man at whose gate Lazarus sat is sent to Hades, a place of torment.

Could this just be another "story" used by Jesus to explain some spiritual concept using symbolism? Was Jesus utilizing an allegoric story to teach people about greed rather than about hell? This is very possible since this was a well-known story given a distinctive twist by Jews.

In Matthew 25, Jesus tells the parable of the talents which describes three servants. Each is given a certain amount of money. One servant receives five talents; the second is given two talents while the last servant receives one talent. The master gives the money to each man according to their abilities.

The first two servants double their money while the servant who is given only one talent does nothing with his share. Instead, he takes his one talent and buries it. The master returns and is happy with the first two servants. He invites them to share in his happiness.

However, he calls the last servant, who buried his talent and did nothing with his share, a worthless servant and proceeds to throw him outside into the darkness where there is "weeping and gnashing of teeth" (Matthew 25:26–30). In this passage, Jesus never mentions fire and brimstone.

Further down in the chapter 25, we read the parable of the sheep and the goats. Jesus says to the goats, "Depart from me, you who are cursed, into the eternal fire prepared for the devil and his angels.... Then they will go away to eternal punishment, but the righteous to eternal life." Through this passage, Jesus makes it clear that the eternal fire was made for the devil and his angels, otherwise known as demons. Does this mean that the punishment of unredeemed people continues eternally or that the *punishment exists eternally* and that those who are punished are punished for an allotted time before being eternally destroyed?

A person believing in the annihilation of the body and soul would ask: If eternal life is a gift, why would God give the same gift to those going to hell so that they can be tortured forever? When God gave us his grace, he says that "the wages of sin is death, but the gift of God is eternal life in Christ Jesus our Lord" (Romans 6:23). In every scripture that Paul writes in the book of Romans, he compares a life of sin as earning death while the gift of God's grace is eternal life. This death might possibly be spiritual death, not physical death; in other words, the death of our body and soul for eternity or its final destruction. Why would he speak only of physical death, as the righteous and unrighteous alike will experience this type of death? Therefore, it is immortality vs. mortality rather than eternal bliss vs. eternal punishment. Consider the following passage from the writings of Paul:

> He will punish those who do not know God and do not obey the gospel of our Lord Jesus. They will be punished

> with everlasting destruction and shut out from the presence
> of the Lord and from the majesty of his power on the day
> he comes to be glorified in his holy people and to be mar-
> veled at among all those who have believed. This includes
> you, because you believed our testimony to you.
> (2 Thessalonians 1:8-10)

At the same time, a person believing in the traditional perspective would refer to the fact that Jesus made it clear how sinners were
thrown into the fiery furnace where there will be weeping and
gnashing of teeth. They would assert that there is no verse support-
ing the fact that this punishment is temporary or for a fixed amount
of time:

> "Just as the weeds are sorted out and burned in the fire, so
> it will be at the end of the world. The Son of Man will send
> his angels, and they will remove from his Kingdom every-
> thing that causes sin and all who do evil. And the angels
> will throw them into the fiery furnace, where there will be
> weeping and gnashing of teeth. Then the righteous will
> shine like the sun in their Father's Kingdom. Anyone with
> ears to hear should listen and understand!" (Matthew
> 13:40-43, NLT)

Whatever we may decide about the nature of hell, we must
always remember two things:

1. As Christians, we must be confident in God's grace. Through
    him, we have the strength to overcome unnecessary guilt and
    fear that may otherwise paralyze us in our faith. God knows
    all of our weaknesses and our strengths. In the end, we are
    saved by grace and not through our acts of righteousness.
    Moreover, our righteous acts should come from an overflow
    of our gratitude for his grace, not from an effort to earn it.

For sin shall not be your master, because you are not under
law, but under grace. (Romans 6:14)

2. Hell always means separation from God for eternity and
brings man face-to-face with the life and meaning he was
created to have. The spiritual world will be revealed to him,
and he will realize that he made the wrong choice, and that
that choice will have eternal consequences. The effect of this
realization will be agonizing.

3
WHY WOULD A LOVING GOD CREATE HELL?

Righteousness and justice are the foundation of your
throne;
love and faithfulness go before you.

Psalm 89:14

Through God's infinite wisdom and justice, God created hell. He
did not create it for people who would one day sin against him, but
rather for the devil and his angels. The Bible mentions how the devil
and the false prophet will be tormented in hell:

And the devil, who deceived them, was thrown into the
lake of burning sulfur, where the beast and the false
prophet had been thrown. They will be tormented day
and night for ever and ever. (Revelation 20:10)

On the other hand, the fact is that everyone deserves to go to
hell—not just the Beast. The Bible clearly says that there is "no one
righteous, not even one" (Romans 3:23). When we compare our
lives to the holiness of God, we will always fall short. God is the
embodiment of everything good and pure. When we sin, we are
breaking the laws that God has set up for his people. There is no

human being on earth who is faultless or above reproach in following God's righteous decrees.

> If you really keep the royal law found in Scripture, "Love
> your neighbor as yourself," you are doing right. But if you
> show favoritism, you sin and are convicted by the law as
> lawbreakers. For whoever keeps the whole law and yet
> stumbles at just one point is guilty of breaking all of it.
> (James 2:8–10)

The above scripture tells us plainly that even if we follow the
whole law but miss one part, we become guilty of breaking all of it.
There is no escape from the fact that we are all lawbreakers. As lawbreakers of God's righteous laws, we need Jesus in our lives. Without
his sacrifice, we would be objects of God's wrath (Romans 5:9,
Ephesians 5:6). But God loved all of mankind enough to send his
Son so that all of us may have a chance to be redeemed. It is only
through God's grace and forgiveness that we are able to wash away
our sins and be justified in his sight. We each have a choice to accept
his grace or not.

Sadly, some still reject his truth and continue to live apart from
God. God is righteous. He cannot leave sin unpunished. He created
a punishment for lawbreakers. This punishment is hell. Some of us
may feel that it is a bit harsh on God's part to have such a punishment, but God calls it justice.

> He will judge your people in *righteousness*,
>   your afflicted ones with *justice*.
> (Psalm 72:2, emphasis added)

At the end of each of our lives, God reassures us that we will be
judged impartially (1 Peter 1:17). There will be no favoritism on
Judgment Day—a comfort for some and a source of fear for others.
The foundation of his throne is love and faithfulness, giving justice

to his afflicted ones. God will judge his people in complete right-eousness. No judge on this earth can claim to be able to do that.

When we think of the fact that hell is final and eternal separa-tion from God, we realize that it exists because no evil can be in the presence of God. The very nature of God repels sin. That is why only those who are forgiven by the sacrifice of Jesus will be able to stand in God's presence.

> If we deliberately keep on sinning after we have received the knowledge of the truth, no sacrifice for sins is left, but only a fearful expectation of judgment and of raging fire that will consume the enemies of God. (Hebrews 10:26-27)

What if we are in the middle of a sinful thought and get run over by a car, will we go straight to hell? Of course not. Does that mean that if we have a bad week during which time we did not have a lot of faith that we are no longer saved? By no means. Our status of sal-vation does not change from moment to moment. The scripture in Hebrews is referring to a continual and deliberate pattern of sin (in the case of the Hebrews, deliberately leaving Jesus and going back to Judaism).

Understanding hell and God's purposes for it can help us to be more confident in this world, especially when this earthly home deals with us unfairly. When we are afflicted and treated unjustly, we can be sure that God will right the wrong. He will be faithful to those who are faithful to him. For many of us, it can be hard to wait on God to make things right as we are impatient beings. Judgment Day can seem too long a delay.

In reality, life is short. Whether you have months or decades yet to live, when you compare it to eternity, it is just a fleeting moment, much like the flash of a camera. We live life as if it will last forever, but the true "forever" comes after this one. Despite this truth, many people in this world live for the here and now. And their thinking influences us. Yet, if we were to simply pierce the veil of their lives, we would see that many of those same neighbors and co-workers feel as though they are living in hell right now. Their lives are a mess—full of pain and sorrow, mostly as a result of their own sins.

4
SO WHAT IF THERE IS A HELL?

On September 11, 2001, the lives of Americans were indelibly scarred with the event of both World Trade Center buildings being destroyed by terrorist plane attacks. Hundreds and thousands of families were affected by the deaths of the victims who were inside the planes and the buildings during the attacks. At the same time, there were untold numbers of heroic acts performed by the citizens of New York who were near or inside the building. They sacrificed their lives to help someone they barely knew or did not know at all.

During their last few minutes, these victims made a split-second decision to risk death so that another human being could go on living. Whether it was to carry someone down the stairs and go up to find another, or to simply help a disabled person down the steps when it slowed progress, these individuals whose names we will never know or remember, made a difference in someone else's life. To this day, even the people who were saved do not know the names of the ones who rescued them.

In the same way, we have all been saved by a man whom we have never met. Even if we were to meet him today by some road, we would not recognize him. Yet, by his grace, Jesus Christ loved us and sacrificed his life for each of us so that we would never have to face the gates of hell.

For this reason, if we know that there is a hell and that it truly exists, we have a choice. We can walk away knowing this and do nothing about it. Or we can take our convictions and begin to make a difference in someone else's life. It is not an easy decision for us to speak up to another person and warn them about the consequences of their soul, but God gives us that choice.

In fact, if someone had predicted that both World Trade Centers were about to be destroyed, very few people would have responded or evacuated the buildings. They probably would have thought that the individual who was warning them was having delusional thoughts. Actually, on that day, even with the warning alarms, people remained in their offices working until they saw the fire and smoke on their floor.

If we believe God's teachings and are committed to them, then we cannot just live life as if nothing will happen. God calls us to become watchmen who help to warn the people. After hearing God's truth, our lives should be altered and changed forever. How we live, how we think and how we feel about others should be transformed. We should be motivated by the love of Christ to save others (2 Corinthians 5:15–21).

Many of us who are Christians have most likely shared our faith with others and have had people make fun of our beliefs. Much as in the days of Noah when he tried to warn the people about the coming of the flood that would destroy the earth, we, too, carry a very serious message which might sound ludicrous to others. Certainly, none of us can predict the future, but we can be certain of God's truth and his word. And he does not lie.

When I first understood that I was not saved, I became alarmed. But what frightened me the most was realizing how many people I knew who needed to hear the same message of God. I did not want them to miss out on God's incredible grace. It motivated me to become a Christian then share my faith with others—first with my family then with all my friends. Consider the following passages:

"Son of man, I have made you a watchman for the house of Israel; so hear the word I speak and give them warning from me. When I say to the wicked, 'O wicked man, you will surely die,' and you do not speak out to dissuade him from his ways, that wicked man will die for his sin, and I will hold you accountable for his blood. But if you do warn the wicked man to turn from his ways and he does not do so, he will die for his sin, but you will have saved yourself." (Ezekiel 33:7-9)

For this is what the Lord has commanded us:

"'I have made you a light for the Gentiles,
    that you may bring salvation to the ends of the
        earth.'"

When the Gentiles heard this, they were glad and honored the word of the Lord; and all who were appointed for eternal life believed. (Acts 13:47-48)

While many Christians view sharing their faith as a burden, the first century Christians believed it to be an honor to be appointed for eternal life and to bring the message to others. Six or seven hundred years previous to that, God spoke to Ezekiel, the prophet, and told him that he would be accountable for the blood of those he did not warn. Though we do not earn our salvation by sharing our faith, God gives us opportunities to help others. We must make the decision to have the heart to care.

Though you have not seen him, you love him; and even though you do not see him now, you believe in him and are filled with an inexpressible and glorious joy, for you are receiving the goal of your faith, the salvation of your souls. (1 Peter 1:8-9)

At the same time, the goal of our faith is not to become a perfect person—nor is it to have the greatest number of converts or to be at every church service. Our goal is not even to give tons of money to the church and to the poor. The goal of our faith is simply to be faithful to God right here and now in his kingdom and continue that relationship for eternity. In the process, wouldn't it be wonderful to bring as many people as possible with us as well?

The fact is that God does not want anyone to experience hell. He went to great lengths to make sure that people would respond to the message of grace. Sending his Son to this earth to be tortured and killed was no little act. It was the greatest sacrifice that anyone could ever make for another. God did this to make a big point: He doesn't want anyone going to hell.

The Christians in the book of Acts were glad and honored to have the word of the Lord and preached the Word to all the people. God blessed the church with amazing expansion to different regions and countries. In much the same way, Ezekiel became one of the greatest prophets of all time, because he took the responsibility to warn the people.

Not all of us are great speakers or teachers, but we can make a difference in the lives of those we love—not with our eloquence or incredible knowledge of the Bible, but rather with our love for them. We are not all chosen to serve in the ministry or to move to a different country as missionaries, but God has chosen us to be his children. And, in turn, we can pass on this special gift to others, whether at work, school or in our neighborhoods.

Personally, I am grateful that Toshiko shared her near-death experience with me. That image has been imprinted in my heart as a warning so that I will be motivated to help others. In the same way, let us allow our light to shine in this dark world and make a difference for someone we love deeply. As God said through Ezekiel, we can say to others:

Rid yourselves of all the offenses you have committed, and get a new heart and a new spirit. Why will you die, O house of Israel? For I take no pleasure in the death of anyone, declares the Sovereign Lord. Repent and live! (Ezekiel 18:31-32)

ಲ

STUDY QUESTIONS

Hell: Is There Really a Place of Condemnation?

1. I presented two views that Christians have of hell. From our limited view right now, none of us knows for sure exactly what hell is like. But there are some things that we can know for sure from Scripture. What are some of those things? How does your view of hell affect your attitude toward God?

2. God is a just God. The world, on the other hand, is full of injustices. How does understanding God's ultimate justice help you to find peace in this life? Have there been times when you have seen God work in this world to bring about justice in your life or in those close to you?

3. In view of this study, what were some of the false perceptions that you had about hell? Where did those views come from? How did the Scriptures help you to see God's perspective better? How does understanding the biblical viewpoint of hell allow your faith to be stronger?

4. Who would you like to reach out to this year and help? Think about ways you can be a light in their lives.

9

Heaven

Is It All That It's Built Up to Be?

> He replied, "You are permitted to understand the secrets of the Kingdom of Heaven, but others are not. To those who listen to my teaching, more understanding will be given, and they will have an abundance of knowledge. But for those who are not listening, even what little understanding they have will be taken away from them.
>
> Matthew 13:11-12 (NLT)

1
Putting Our Hope in Heaven

Dear sisters, our spiritual journey through these pages is almost over. The final stop in our adventure takes us to our ultimate destination—heaven. As Christians, we not only have this hope, but we have the secrets of the kingdom of heaven. Through suffering and difficulty; joy and victory, at the end of our lives, we will all face God. What a day of rejoicing it will be for those of us who have lived for our Lord! Ultimately, heaven is the goal for the faithful. The journey on the way will take us to the very limits of that which we can endure. At the same time, God will provide us with just the right amount of encouragement and love to help us make it through.

Is heaven real to you? Have you ever tried to imagine what it might be like? Do you look forward to heaven, or are you too busy to think about it? Unfortunately, many of us are focused on the "here and now," and we rarely allow our minds to ponder heaven with all of its glory and majesty. Life moves too fast—with each of us running to keep up. Who has time to wonder about heaven, right? After retirement, maybe, but not right now.

No, my friends, it is important to think about heaven today. It is never too early to look forward to heaven and the blessings that await us there.

Think about what motivates you to work hard every day. Are you dreaming of that cruise you have always wanted to take? Is all your daily sacrifice in order to get a nice retirement? Do you push yourself to work overtime for that dream home? Do you slave for your boss with the hope of being able to purchase that new car?

Well, you are not alone. Those dreams and hopes are necessary to propel you to give your best when it gets tough. Without those dreams and desires, you would never make the sacrifices and the effort.

Now, imagine heaven for a moment. Streets of gold. Gates of pearls. The pavement decorated with emeralds, sapphires, rubies and diamonds—and even some stones that I've never heard of. Your dream home sits up on that hill or beach, with all the amenities, no expenses spared. There's a big chair next to God especially for you, so that you can talk to him whenever you want. No more tears. No more suffering. No more death. Jesus is right there to give you a squeeze every time you need a big bear hug. No more stress. No more traffic to fight. No more boss yelling at you for all your mistakes. There is just peace and harmony everywhere.

The sacrifices that you made are stored up in your heavenly bank account. No matter what your bank account looks like here, the one up there is looking really good. The joint and back pains will never return, and you will be able not only to walk and run, but also jump and fly without ever getting tired! Dieting to lose weight? No more! The delicious banquet at God's table will have no calories! And forget about all those tiring workouts to keep yourself in shape. They're all gone. You will have a beautiful spiritual body!

This is real heaven! This hope is more genuine and realistic than your dream home or your retirement plan, which do not always work out the way we think. If we could truly put our hope in heaven, then we would be motivated to do extraordinary things. God tells us about heaven throughout the Scriptures. The images above are not something that I just made up. They are based on actual passages in God's word. Of course all the descriptions are symbolic. But they are employed by God to let us know that heaven will be so very special, so very amazing, so very over the top, so very full of treasures. In fact, when Jesus taught about heaven, he spoke in parables using treasure and pearls to show how much we should value the heavenly kingdom that God has prepared for us.

> "The kingdom of heaven is like treasure hidden in a field. When a man found it, he hid it again, and then in his joy went and sold all he had and bought that field.
>
> "Again, the kingdom of heaven is like a merchant looking for fine pearls. When he found one of great value, he went away and sold everything he had and bought it."
> (Matthew 13:44-46)

To the man or woman who really understands the kingdom of heaven, there will be no price too high to pay for that gift which Jesus compares to a treasure or fine pearls. Even in the Old Testament, Malachi writes to the Jews about giving their best to God. God tells his people to test him and that he would throw open the floodgates of heaven with so much blessing that they would have no room for it (Malachi 3:10). In other words, heaven is full of blessings—far more than we could even imagine.

Those angels are waiting to greet us. Jesus anticipates welcoming us with open arms, and he stands ready to tell us: "Well done! Good and faithful servant!" The most wonderful part is that it will last for all of eternity!

Hope like this can carry us through the darkest and most hopeless times. As I shared in the previous chapter, my lupus was officially declared in remission in 1995. However, in 2002, I went to the doctor's office for my yearly check-up only to find out that my lupus was active again. For someone like me, I need this eternal hope to keep fighting discouragement and disappointment. Just when I had thought that I had won this battle, Satan once again began to tempt me with worry and despair. What I have learned through all of this is not to put my eyes on my situation but to put my hope in Jesus and on heaven. Jesus focused on the joy set before him as he endured the cross (Hebrews 12:1–2). What was the joy set before him? Heaven, of course! It helped him to make it without sinning! Wow!

Losing hope causes us to grow weary. It drains us of our desire to do what is right. When we are not motivated, we lose what precious faith we have. Hope is what brings joy into our lives especially when situations are grim. Dear sisters, heaven is waiting for us with an amazing reward. God wants us to make it to the very end. He does not want us to miss out on the wonderful blessings that await us there.

> From heaven the LORD looks down
> and sees all mankind;
> from his dwelling place he watches
> all who live on earth—
> he who forms the heart of all,
> who considers everything they do.
> No king is saved by the size of his army;
> no warrior escapes by his great strength.
> A horse is vain hope for deliverance;

despite all its great strength it cannot save.
But the eyes of the LORD are on those who fear him,
    on those whose hope is in his unfailing love,
to deliver them from death
    and keep them alive in famine.

We wait in hope for the LORD;
    he is our help and our shield.
In him our hearts rejoice,
    for we trust in his holy name.
May your unfailing love rest upon us, O LORD,
    even as we put our hope in you.
(Psalm 33:13-22)

There are many scriptures describing how the Lord will take care of us when we put our hope in him. The hope we have is spiritual and not of this physical world, which is hope that finds its security in jobs, education and homes. Without the priority on God, these aspects of our lives only lead to disappointment and disillusionment. Think about the number of people who look for love and fulfillment in marriage and end up in divorce. Look at the many parents who put all their hope in their children only to experience disappointment and failure.

No matter what we do, we will face frustration and defeat in our lives. The people who we love are not perfect. The jobs that we depend on will not always last. The boyfriends that we date will not give us the fulfillment we seek. So how do we cope with the reality around us as we wait for heaven?

From ancient times, people had a belief in heaven or of an afterlife that would be better than the life on this earth. They stayed faithful during the tough times in the hopes of a better place after death. In fact, the ancient Egyptians believed that heaven was actually a physical place beyond the stars in the heavens in a "dark area" of space.[1] From Hinduism to Judaism, the concept of being a "good" person in order to attain paradise is taught. Interestingly, Roman Catholics believe that you go through a "purgatory" after death where "lesser" sins can be cleansed before entering into heaven.

The Bible teaches that it is only through Christ and his grace that we are able to enter into heaven. No "good" deeds are sufficient enough to earn our salvation. Regardless of how many virtuous deeds we accumulate, it will never be enough. Rather, our good works should come from an overflow of gratitude *for* our salvation, not to earn it. We should not be driving ourselves into the ground to somehow "make it into heaven." Heaven can never be bought or earned. It is purely a gift from God. There is not one human being who is worthy to receive eternal life—no matter how many good works anyone has done.

> No man can redeem the life of another
> > or give to God a ransom for him—
> The ransom for a life is costly,
> > no payment is ever enough—
> that he should live on forever
> > and not see decay.
>
> But God will redeem my life from the grave;
> > He will surely take me to himself.
> (Psalm 49:7-9, 15)

Only God can redeem our soul from the grave. Only Jesus can save us from the consequence of our sins. Our hope is found in God alone. No matter what is happening in our lives, we have a true hope before us. If Jesus was motivated by the hope that was before him, how much more should we be excited about the promise of salvation before us? Let us renew our conviction about heaven and its blessings as we continue to read the following pages.

2

HEAVEN IS A REAL PLACE

> And I heard a loud voice from the throne saying, "Now the dwelling of God is with men, and he will live with them. They will be his people, and God himself will be with them and be their God. He will wipe every tear from their eyes. There will be no more death or mourning or crying or pain, for the old order of things has passed away." (Revelation 21:3-4)

The Bible says that heaven is a place with no more death or mourning or crying or pain. In the Scriptures, God describes heaven as his dwelling place where men will live with him for eternity. Even as Jesus was hanging from the cross, he spoke of heaven to the thief next to him, who, at the end of his life, feared God. Jesus promised the thief that he would be with him in Paradise that very day.

The apostle Paul enjoyed preaching and teaching about heaven; he mentions it numerous times in his writings as we have read earlier. He had personal experiences of being "caught up" in the third heaven. He went into Paradise and heard things that he was not permitted to tell (2 Corinthians 12:2–4).

Most likely, as a result of that encounter, he struggled with wanting to depart from his physical body to be with Christ, but remained for the sake of the Christians (Philippians 1:22–25). That must have been very difficult for Paul to see a glimpse of heaven and then have to return to his life of persecution and prison.

A few years ago, I visited Rome, Italy, where I toured the Coliseum. In the first century, Christians were tortured and killed as entertainment in that arena. I also walked inside the catacombs where Christians lived in holes in the ground—among dead bodies—to escape the persecution of the time. Imagine taking your children to live in utter darkness and sleeping beside decaying bodies, because you did not want to renounce your faith. If heaven is not a real place, these people suffered and died for nothing.

When we learn to see heaven as these great men and women of faith did, the manner in which we live on this earth will be transformed. Our perspective on life will be different. What used to mean everything to us will mean nothing from the perspective of eternity. In fact, we will start to value the things that God values, and not what this world values. We will make different decisions—sacrificing more than ever before—to seek treasures that are not of this world.

In the book of Hebrews, God explains how all the men and women of faith were longing for a better country—a heavenly one (Hebrews 11:16). They were not ashamed of their God and were willing to endure being stoned, imprisoned and flogged for the sake of heaven. They lived in caves, deserts, mountains and in holes in the ground for their faith, so that they could see their heavenly home. They were waiting for a better place where they would be able to rest. And this new resting place would be spacious and open— much larger than the catacombs, holes and caves in which the early Christians lived—a true paradise.

> The angel who talked with me had a measuring rod of gold to measure the city, its gates and its walls. The city was laid out like a square, as long as it was wide. He measured the city with the rod and found it to be 12,000 stadia in length, and as wide and high as it is long. He measured its wall and it was 144 cubits thick, by man's measurement, which the angel was using. (Revelation 21:15-17)

As the angel shows the apostle John the New Jerusalem, he takes out a measuring stick made of gold and measures this amazing place. The city was shaped like a cube with 2220 kilometers or 1380 miles on each side. What does this mean in terms of area? It is estimated that even if only twenty-five percent of the space were used for dwelling in, twenty billion people could be accommodated spaciously![2] If this is true, then the world's population, at present, being almost seven billion, would have more than enough space in heaven. And since we know that down through the ages, only a few have chosen to go the narrow way, there will be plenty of space for everyone.

Of course, we know that John's Revelation is a writing that employs symbolism to help us realize the glory and the magnitude of heaven and of God's presence. Therefore, we can't know the literal size of heaven. But in the passage God is letting us know that it is expansive.

Having lived in New York City, Tokyo, Bangkok and Paris, I know what it is to have very limited living space. The rent for even a small apartment in each of these cities is astronomical! Personal space, even in the home, is a grand luxury. When our family moved to Denver, Colorado, that was what hit us first—vast skies and open space everywhere. Living in the suburbs of Denver, I am experiencing a taste of what heaven must be like. Every morning I can see the Rocky Mountains and enjoy so much breathing space in my comfortable home.

Heaven will afford plenty of freedom to roam about. It would probably take all of eternity to explore every nook and cranny there. Dear sisters, how exciting it will be to see and to discover the different places in God's heaven. If we think that the earth with its scenery is remarkable, we will be in greater awe and wonder at the beauty of paradise! We will be in constant amazement as we discover even more magnificent creations of God. Forget rainbows and beaches—there will probably be rainbow colored skies and beaches on mountain tops! Whatever we could imagine, whatever we would desire to see, God will just make it happen because it's heaven!

While we are alive in this world, however, we must face the fact of life's reality as well. There is much poverty, hunger, crime, injustice and evil. We can allow these "realities" to make us feel disillusioned. We might even look at our own lives and become discontent with what God has given us. As we deal with the "realities" of this world, let us not allow them to cloud the vision of what God has prepared for us. For now, we can embrace the priceless lessons that they teach us.

My family and I were deeply impacted during one trip to the Philippines. My husband, my children and I decided to volunteer to help the poor. There, along with other volunteers, we visited a garbage dump where the poorest people of Manila lived. The place was called "Smoky Mountain"—a mountain of garbage slowly burning every day causing smoke to rise constantly from that area. The neighborhood carried such a strong stench that it caused some people in our group to feel nauseated and almost faint. Those individuals had to remain on the bus and could not continue into the site. The odor came from decomposing garbage. There were so many flies and insects that it was almost unbearable. And, the heat and humidity was incredibly intense.

The volunteers had packed their backpacks full of toothbrushes, toothpaste, soap and other toiletries to give to the people living there. They were so happy to receive these small commodities. They thanked all of us volunteers over and over again. Some of the people even invited us into their very modest and small homes, made with rubbish. Our hearts were cut to see the joy of these people. None of us American volunteers had ever seen people dwelling in such deplorable circumstances. Each of us went home with the decision to never complain again about what we had or did not have.

Worldly possessions at any level are important to us. We, as women, think we need certain effects to survive and also to be happy. We like to have our favorite drinks, our special shampoo, our beloved chair or spot to sit in and our particular shops to buy our necessities from. Not all of us are that fussy about the things that we need, but we certainly do have our preferences and desires. They may not necessarily be bad desires but can influence our mood and our happiness, depending on whether we are able to fulfill those needs in our heart.

God wants us to be content with what we have and to look forward to all that he has prepared for us in our eternal home. Whether we live with very little or with plenty, this world is temporal. None of our homes, our clothes, our jobs or life, as we know it, will last. As we live this short life, we can be confident of a place waiting for us. Life is a blink of an eye in comparison to eternity. Let us not allow our temporal surroundings to dictate our perception of heaven. Heaven is more real than all of these things. And when we get to heaven, we will all laugh at the silly ways we yearned for the things of this world!

> The world and its desires pass away, but the man who does the will of God lives forever. (1 John 2:17)

3

UNDERSTANDING THE CONCEPT OF ETERNITY

> He has made everything beautiful in its time. He has also set eternity in the hearts of men; yet they cannot fathom what God has done from beginning to end. (Ecclesiastes 3:11)

Forever is a long time. Living somewhere for all of eternity is a concept that is difficult for us to grasp. Heaven must be the most amazing place for it to be paradise for forever and never lose its wonder. Otherwise, we would get bored and frustrated knowing that we were stuck somewhere forever. Nonetheless, as it states in the scripture above, somewhere in our hearts, we long for eternity, because God has placed that desire there. For this reason, without understanding why, people throughout history have sought to find the fountain of youth or a paradise where no one would ever grow old. There are even books written about secret places where a sip of rejuvenating waters can give eternal life. Unfortunately, in reality, there is no such fountain, and no one can live forever—at least not in this world.

God, however, offers us eternal life. As Christians, we can look forward to eternity as the greatest spiritual gift. Death will not be an end for us but a great victory! Death has no control over us and is actually a window or a gateway to our eternal home. This is a great mystery for every follower of Jesus. Because there is nothing on this earth that is close to lasting forever, no one can truly comprehend eternity until we see God.

This is why people around us tend to grab for the temporal rather for the eternal. And, we, as Christians, can get caught up in the same trap. No wonder we have such a hard time grasping the concept of heaven. But God is an eternal God. He has no beginning and no end. The Bible says that he *is* the Alpha and the Omega—the beginning and the end (Revelation 21:6). To understand God is to gain some insight into God's timeless nature. As a matter of fact, many of the scriptures that refer to God describe this characteristic of being eternal—his love, his glory, his wisdom, his power, his blessings, his righteousness and so on (Psalms 21:6, 1 Kings 10:9, Romans 1:20, 1 Peter 5:10).

Therefore, it is only through God that we can finally achieve true immortality. There is no other force or being who has the capacity to grant everlasting life. The God of heaven and earth is the only eternal being in existence who can bless us with such a gift.

The psalmist says:

Your throne was established long ago;
you are from all eternity. (Psalm 93:2)

God's throne has been established from long ago. The very nature of God is eternal—he defines *eternity*. When we look at God, we see a divine being who is everlasting; he has been and will always be. Even as Jesus spoke to God right before going to the cross, he looked toward heaven and prayed: "Now, this is eternal life: that they may know you, the only true God, and Jesus Christ, whom you have sent" (John 17:3). In other words, knowing this great God is having eternal life. Wow, that is encouraging—because we have a relationship with this eternal being!

It is no wonder that the apostles of Christ and many other heroes of faith risked their lives to communicate to the world about the good news of Jesus. Most of them died trying to help others to see the truth. The apostle, Paul, said that for him, "to live is Christ and to die is gain" (Philippians 1:21). He understood that nothing in this life compared to being with Jesus forever. Repeatedly, Paul would share how he would rather die and go be with God than to live in this world (2 Corinthians 5:8). He had already gotten a taste of heaven. This world was not his home. His relationship with the Lord was everything to him. Although it was a mystery to him as well, he was confident in the glory that awaited him after his death. For Paul, heaven was the greatest victory. Being with his Lord for all eternity was the goal of his life.

In his attempt to preach this good news to others, Paul lived like a "fool for Christ" (1 Corinthians 4:10). He lived on public display like men condemned to die in the arena. He was hungry, thirsty, in rags, brutally treated and homeless—all for the sake of the gospel. He had become the scum of the earth, the refuse of the world (1 Corinthians 4:13).

He recounted his sufferings for the sake of the gospel. He had endured beatings, floggings, shipwrecks, dangers from false brothers and Gentiles, and imprisonment (2 Corinthians 11:23–27). He was a man who lived on the edge so that he could bring as many as possible with him to heaven. Look at what Paul says to the church in Corinth:

> But let me tell you something wonderful, a mystery I'll probably never fully understand. We're not all going to die—but we are all going to be changed. You hear a blast to end all blasts from a trumpet, and in the time that you look up and blink your eyes—it's over. On signal from that trumpet from heaven, the dead will be up and out of their graves, beyond the reach of death, never to die again. At the same moment and in the same way, we'll all be changed. In the resurrection scheme of things, this has to happen: everything perishable taken off the shelves and replaced by the imperishable, this mortal replaced by the immortal. Then the saying will come true:
>
> Death swallowed by triumphant Life!
> Who got the last word, oh, Death?
> Oh, Death, who's afraid of you now?
>
> It was sin that made death so frightening and law-code guilt that gave sin leverage, its destructive power. But now in a single victorious stroke of Life, all three—sin, guilt, death—are all gone, the gift of our Master, Jesus Christ. Thank God! (1 Corinthians 15:51-57, The Message)

Paul lived in the danger zone every day because he understood eternity with God. Just reading the scripture above in everyday language makes immortality seem so clear and real. Our bodies are ephemeral and transitory. Our spirit and our resurrected bodies, however, will be immortal. In fact, our souls have been stamped with the seal of the Holy Spirit which is a guarantee for eternal life with God (2 Corinthians 5:5). We will be transformed from the perishable to the imperishable. For when the last trumpet sounds, we will rise as immortal beings.

Death will have lost its sting. The sting of death is sin. It will no longer have power over us. Nothing in all of creation will be able to prevent us from rising up to be with our Lord! Satan and death will be powerless in our lives. We will have already won the final victory in our lives. Our fleshly desires with which we fought daily will be gone. There will be no more darkness or sin in our lives. All the effort we put into fighting Satan's temptations will be worth it. Light will have triumphed over darkness forever!

Paul spoke about the promise that lay before him as being his *eternal* reward. If there was no heaven, no forgiveness of sins and no resurrection, then Paul should have been pitied over all men, as he would have wasted his life for nothing (1 Corinthians 15:19).

Yet, he asserted that heaven was real. The resurrection of Jesus was a fact—not a myth or a made-up story. For this reason, our sins will cease to exist. Our guilt will vanish. Even our mistakes and our failings will be forgotten—taken away forever. All that we had feared and that had caused us pain will evaporate when we rise from the dead. The cost? There was none in Paul's mind; he was getting the better end of the deal. This life possessed nothing of value in comparison to what lay ahead of him:

> But whatever was to my profit I now consider a loss for the sake of Christ. What is more, I consider everything a loss compared to the surpassing greatness of knowing Christ Jesus my Lord, for whose sake I have lost all things. I consider them rubbish, that I may gain Christ.
> (Philippians 3:7-8)

Paul saw his life as "rubbish" in comparison to gaining Christ.

Paul's attitude towards eternity can help us to see the next world in a better light. He understood that this world was fleeting (2 Corinthians 4:18). The unseen part of his life was eternal. He gave up living in the "comfort" zone, and poured out his life as a drink offering for the sake of the gospel. His sacrifices did not make sense to those in the world. He called others to give 100%—just like his Lord did on the cross. He was convinced that there was a crown awaiting him—a crown that would last forever (1 Corinthians 9:25). In view of this, he became a slave to the gospel (1 Corinthians 9:19). How many of us think this way anymore?

Dear sisters, is the picture getting clearer to you? Is heaven becoming more real? Are you getting excited about the thought of "forever"? After years of not living in the "comfort zone," Paul was eager to experience eternal comfort and joy. His difficulties in this life were worth the reward that was waiting for him in heaven. He looked forward to eternity more than anything.

Having an eternal perspective will teach us to cherish what is most important in this life—having a relationship with our Lord and Savior and teaching others about him as well. This was how Paul lived during his short life on this earth. He wanted to know Christ and the power of his resurrection. He wanted to have fellowship with Jesus through participating in the same sufferings, and somehow attain to the resurrection from the dead (Philippians 3:10–11). He was certain that his citizenship was in heaven, not on earth (Phippians 3:20). He knew, without a doubt, that his "lowly body" would be like Christ's glorious body (Philippians 3:21). What was going to help him get there? Living by faith and having the goal to please God (2 Corinthians 5:7–9).

Since Christ's resurrection is real, we can be sure of the genuineness of our own personal resurrection into God's presence and heaven. Our bodies are only jars of clay, temporary tents, according to the apostle Paul (2 Corinthians 4:7, 5:1–5). The true life that will be revealed in our body will come from the power of God. As we give ourselves over to death for the sake of Jesus Christ, our bodies will be given over to life in Christ (2 Corinthians 4:11). This is understanding eternity in this world.

> Now to the King eternal, immortal, invisible, the only God, be honor and glory for ever and ever. Amen. (1 Timothy 1:17)

4

WAIT FOR GOD'S PROMISES

Do you remember as a child sitting in the back seat of your parents' car going for a long drive? It took hours to get ready for the trip, and then when all of you finally climbed into the car to drive off, you started to feel bored only after a few minutes. You tried to be quiet for fifteen lo-o-ong minutes; but your little brother started bugging you, and you finally asked, "Are we there yet?" Another grueling ten or fifteen minutes would pass, and this time, you got your little brother to ask, "Are we there yet?" You both took turns asking a few more times, harmless right?

Your parents tried to be nice the first few times and explained to you how long the trip was going to take, but that never stopped you and your little brother from asking the same old question about ten more times during a span of only thirty minutes. The "fun" family vacation didn't sound fun anymore after hearing that you would have to be strapped down next to your little brother for ten hours! This was not what you expected for your vacation. The beach and the amusement park were supposed to be there after ten or fifteen minutes, tops! Who had ever heard of a vacation sitting in the backseat of a car for ten endless hours with your little brother?

Now, let us look at our lives. God is the parent driving the car.

Yes, twenty years of hard work is a long time; twelve years of schooling plus college seems like eternity! Living in the same old house for ten years is frustrating when you want that other home in the next neighborhood! God keeps driving the old car with us in the backseat, as we wait and wonder.

Yes, just like small children, we get impatient with God. We feel like there are so many delays to this "nice" life as Christians. We thought that God was supposed to bless our lives. Where was the reward on earth? Of course, we know that paradise awaits us in heaven, but we have been "good" here on earth. We should get something for that, right? Then, we pray to God. He tells us to wait. We pray again. He makes us wait even longer. Suddenly, we want to break out of our seat belts and get there on our own. Bad idea.

Dear sisters, as much as we want to deny it, God knows where he is taking us and what he is doing with our lives. All along the way, God keeps looking back at us sitting in the back seat. He is smiling, sometimes even chuckling. This vacation is going to be truly special. We have no idea how amazing it is going to be. God looks at twenty years as nothing. He even looks at a hundred years as if it were but a second. Our lives, in comparison to eternity, are a flash of light or a twinkle of an eye.

Yet, this life carries many burdens and challenges. From God's perspective, every effort to live godly lives in this depraved world will be worth it. Every act of kindness in return for cruelty is seen. Every effort to forgive evildoers is felt and recognized by God. Every deed of generosity and mercy, left unappreciated, is known in detail by our Lord. Every sacrifice done out of love is honored by God. Every life that is given for the sake of the gospel is glorious in God's sight. Jesus has gone ahead of us. He is waiting to welcome us with open arms. The question is: Will we wait for God to fulfill his promises in our lives? Hear Jesus as he promises to prepare a place for us in his Father's house:

"Do not let your hearts be troubled. Trust in God; trust also in me. In my Father's house are many rooms; if it were not so, I would have told you. I am going there to prepare a place for you. And if I go and prepare a place for you, I will come back and take you to be with me that you also may be where I am." (John 14:1 - 3)

Each of us has a desire inside our hearts that wants to experience heaven, here, not just when we die. In fact, most of us want to live a long life. We want to enjoy being with our family and friends. We want life to the full. Waiting for death seems morbid, dark and even demotivating.

In the meantime, it seems unfair that "evil" men and women seem to have life all together. They are not riding in old cars. They are not strapped in with their seatbelts; they get to jump around in the back seat. Their driver takes them to the spots where they want to go, not these long "ten hour" drives. They even get to stop any-where on the road to buy what they want. The problem with this is that they will never get to their destination.

Remember, God is our driver. He will get us to our destination, safely. The seatbelts may be uncomfortable. The person you are sit-ting next to might not be your number one choice of people to be with. You might even get car sick along the way, but you will get there, because God is a good driver. He knows the best roads for our lives. He takes us on the safest routes. He will stop when we need it the most. He will feed us exactly when we need it. In all of this, God asks us to trust in him and continue to do good (Psalm 37:3).

Whether you are a teenager or past retirement age, eternity is waiting. God has his timing for our lives—it may be long; it may be shorter than we think. Who knows what tomorrow will bring? Who are we to boast about tomorrow (James 4:14)? I have learned from personal experience that no one can predict when he or she will die.

In fact, at every stage of my life, whether during elementary school, college or my young married life, I have lost someone close to me and close to my age as they died an untimely death.

God is the one who holds that verdict in his hands. With all wisdom, our Lord will decide the right time, for each of us.

Until then, the Spirit and the bride say, "Come!" (Revelation 22:17). The waters of life are available to those who thirst and desire the free gift of life. Every day that goes by, we have a choice to continue to follow our God. This world will place a countless number of obstacles in our path. Those hurdles will test our faith to the very edge. Every hero of faith in the Bible faced ordeals beyond human strength.

Will heaven be worth the effort in the end? Of course, it will be. More than that, there will be no regrets as we see God face to face. His light will shine brightly on us. Jesus will be sitting at God's right hand smiling down on us with pride. Their loving embrace will melt away all memories of our hardships. Then, we will know without a shadow of a doubt that our journey is finally over. We will have made it to the goal of our faith—the salvation of our souls (1 Peter 1:9).

I saw this eternal attitude in a very special woman named Irene Gurganus. On April 15, 2006, this woman of faith left to be with her Lord. She knew that she was dying. The doctors had told her that she had anywhere from a day to a year to live. She ended up living ten months after her prognosis. During that brief period of time, I saw her attitude and perspective on life transform. She had always tried to live each day to its full. Yet, during the last few months before her death, every person and every event became a cherished memory for her.

First, she moved from California to Texas in order to be with her oldest daughter. Before her move, she began to give away all her material possessions to the people whom she loved the most. She thought through each of the items she owned and matched them to the receiver. She took the little money she had and made each birthday and every holiday special for her friends and relatives, because she knew that it would be her last chance. As she faced death, she had almost nothing left belonging to her name, except her family and friends. The little money that she kept was intended to be used for her burial so that no one would have to be burdened financially by her passing.

She had come from a wealthy family in Chicago before she gave her life to Christ. Each day that she lived was devoted to helping to see the world won for Jesus. By the time she was eighty-seven, she had lived in many different cities and spent several years on the mission field. She truly understood that she was going to heaven. She was excited to see her husband, George, again. She was confident about death. She had no fear.

My husband and I spent time with her a month before she died. Even during our visit, she gave her very best to us despite her weakened condition. She wanted our memories of her to be special. We talked and laughed and reminisced about the years we spent together. That was the last time we had with her in this life. And we look forward to seeing her again in heaven.

The last day of her life was spent at home with her daughter. As her daughter was resting in her room, Irene was also taking a nap in her favorite chair. As she slept, her eyes were opened to a new world—her eternal home. She did not have to wear the tubes from her oxygen machine any longer. She did not have to use a walker to get up. She was no longer tied to a wheel chair. She was running, jumping and flying to her Lord. She was free! She was young again, bursting with energy—no more pain, no more tears and no more fear.

Sisters, heaven is more real than your dream career. It is more lasting than your brand new home. It is more remarkable than a round-the-world vacation. It is richer than all the treasures of the world. It is more satisfying than the richest of meals. It is more comforting and peaceful than any five-star beachside resort. It is more rewarding than any first prize for a contest or competition. For a

Christian who stays faithful to God until the very end, it will be his or her greatest crown and glory to receive.

Let us make a decision to live each day like it is our last one. Life is truly very short. Let us not waste time worrying and fretting. The minutes and hours will go by so fast. Irene taught me one last lesson. She called our home the day before she passed away. I got busy and thought that I would call her back the next day. She had no next day. To this day I regret not taking the opportunity to call her back right away. I am glad, however, that I will see her again in heaven where she will be waiting for me.

> One thing I ask of the LORD,
>   this is what I seek:
> that I may dwell in the house of the LORD
>   all the days of my life,
> to gaze upon the beauty of the LORD
>   and to seek him in his temple. (Psalm 27:4)

Allow God to be the driver of your life. Enjoy the ride. It will be worth it in the end. It is a blessing to have our God as the protector and guide of our lives. We know the destination. There are no surprises as long as he is in the driver's seat. Don't take off that seatbelt. Don't let those signs along the way convince you to get out. Just "be strong and take heart and wait for the Lord" (Psalm 27:14).

> "Behold, I am coming soon! My reward is with me, and I will give it to everyone according to what he has done. I am the Alpha and the Omega, the first and the last, the Beginning and the End.
> "Blessed are those who wash their robes, that they may have the right to the tree of life and may go through the gates into the city." (Revelation 22:12-14)

෨

Dear sisters, our journey through these pages has come to an end. Have your eyes been opened to see the spiritual world a little bit clearer? Has your faith been encouraged by the Scriptures? Are you ready to step out on faith again having been renewed in your convictions? Are you ready to keep fighting the good fight that Christ has called you to? Are you ready to guard your heart against Satan and fight against his evil schemes?

We must still cross the passage of life before we are face-to-face with our Lord. Let us stand firm, knowing that our Lord and Savior is standing by our side. Every step in this spiritual walk will bring new adventures and intimidating challenges. We are on a journey— being purified, tested and prepared for our final destination. We must complete the course in the labyrinth of life so we can finally go home. In all of this, we need to keep our perspective heavenward. All of your heroes of faith had their eyes focused on heaven as they suffered for God. This motivation drove them to persevere through the toughest times.

You have a heavenly home. It is beautiful—a magnificent place with the best that you can imagine and even more. Jesus will be waiting with open arms to greet you. God will have a special chair prepared for you to sit in so that you can cuddle next to your daddy in heaven and tell him all your feelings and your thoughts. You will laugh and you will smile with so much joy that it will fill your entire soul. And there will be no more tears running down your cheeks because there are none in heaven. Angels will lead you to your treasures. You will leap. You will fly. You will soar. After all the adventures on this earth, you will find rest and peace. Heaven will no longer be just a part of the spiritual world, but it will be your home forever and ever. Amen.

❦

STUDY QUESTIONS

Heaven: Is It All That It's Built Up to Be?

1. Do you believe in the existence of heaven? Is it real to you? What do you put all your hope into as you live each day right now?

2. What can you do to cause heaven to be more real to you?

3. Paul lived as though everything was rubbish in this world. Jesus endured the cross with its shame and scorn for the hope that was before him. Think about the great heroes of faith who suffered in the face of persecution and suffering, not compromising in their faith because of the hope ahead of them. How can we have the same attitude in our walk with the Lord?

4. What are the obstacles in your life that prevent you from putting your hope in heaven?

5. How are you attached to the things of this world?

6. Think about heaven daily for the next week, and imagine that you will be there in just a few days. How will the decisions you make this week be different?

NOTES

Chapter 4—Demons: Are These Evil Spirits Still Active Today?

1. Wikipedia: "Demons"

2. Ibid.

3. Merrill F. Unger, *What Demons Can Do to Saints* (Chicago: Moody Bible Institute, 1991).

Chapter 5—Angels: Are They Truly Around Me?

1. Hugh Ross, Ph.D., M.Sc., "Beyond the Cosmos: Angels, Cherubim, Seraphim and Archangels," navpress.com, 1996. (from Internet Web page on *Angels*)

2. Ibid.

3. Phil Greetham, Rev. "The Nativity Pages," *Web site 2001, www.ourworld.compuserve.com/homepage/p_greetham/wisemen*

4. Roy A. Reinhold, "Exact Date of Yeshua's Birth," Prophecy Truths Web site, February 1, 2001.

5. *Life Application Study Bible, New International Version* (Carol Stream, IL: Tyndale House, 1997), 229.

Chapter 6—Prayer: Why Do It When God Already Knows?

1. Joseph Jacobs and Louis Grey, "Phoenicia," JewishEncyclopedia.com

Chapter 7—God's Church: Why Do I Need Family?

1. Not her real name.

2. Not his real name.

3. Wikipedia: "Kingdom of God"

4. See *One Another: Transformational Relationships in the Body of Christ*, Tom Jones and Steve Brown (Spring Hill, TN: DPI, 2008).

5. Not his real name.

6. James Oliver Horton and Lois E. Horton, *Slavery and the Making of America* (New York: Oxford University Press USA, 2006), 77.

Chapter 8—Hell: Is There Really a Place of Condemnation?

1. Charles Honey, "Belief in Hell Dips, but Some Say They've Already Been There," *Religious News Service*, August 14, 2008.

2. Dante Alighieri, "The Divine Comedy: Inferno," www.everypoet.com/archive/poetry/dante

3. Alice K. Turner, *The History of Hell* (Orlando, FL: Harcourt Brace & Company, 1993), 40.

Chapter 9—Heaven: Is It All That It's Built Up to Be?

1. Wikipedia, "Heaven"

2. *New International Version* footnote, (Grand Rapids: Zondervan, 1978), 1977.